DATE DUE

MAY 28			
JAN 27			
MAY 9			
NOV 2			
OCT 5 1972			
SEP 1 9			
Teacher			
NOV 1 6			
NOV 29 '83			
NOV 1 7 1988			
APR 2 3 1992			
MAY 1 2 1992			
GAYLORD			PRINTED IN U.S.A.

Say It
with Your Camera

An Approach to Creative Photography

by JACOB DESCHIN

New York: A. S. Barnes and Co., Inc.

London: Thomas Yoseloff Ltd.

770

SAY IT WITH YOUR CAMERA
Completely Revised Edition

Library of Congress Catalog Card Number 60-10523

Manufactured in the United States of America

Preface to the Second Edition

THE DECADE THAT has passed since the publication of the first edition of this book has been an eventful one, thanks largely to the invigorating influence of photojournalism and the 35mm camera. However, the problems of the amateur first discussed here continue almost unchanged, especially in the area of the tight little island inhabited by the pictorial salons and the camera clubs.

Nevertheless, and again excluding the latter, which have remained as always almost untouched by general progress in photography as an expressive medium, much new talent has come to the fore and there have been some important innovations in approach. The accelerated interest in color photography and the growing preoccupation of photographers with their status as artists are recognized in two new chapters.

The new edition has been carefully revised and some new material added. With a few exceptions, the original illustrations have been replaced and the total number expanded.

Preface to the First Edition

THIS BOOK is for grownups of all ages. It is written in the belief that amateur photography as a medium of personal expression has now reached maturity. In spite of this coming-of-age, many amateurs continue merely to scratch the surface of their potentialities for saying things with a camera.

The book recognizes that the chief fault of today's amateur photographer is that he places undue stress on the "how" of photography rather than on the "what" and the "why." He is more conscious of camera and materials than he is of his personal reactions as a thoughtful photographer to the subject matter he encounters. The result is that, lacking true inspiration and apparently unaware of the function of the photographer to reveal and to interpret an individual viewpoint, the great bulk of amateur effort is based on imitativeness and the worship of false values.

Photographers can do better. I have written this book because I am convinced they can and because I hope they will —once they have been shown the way.

Part 1, "Picture Your World," tries to help the reader arrive at some idea of why he takes pictures so that he can do something about it. Part 2, "Techniques Are Words," interprets know-how as a creative means of revealing most effectively in a picture the photographer's thinking and feeling about the subject photographed. Part 3, "New Patterns," covers the photographer's environment and tries to show that unless this phase of his day-to-day living and learning harmonizes with his thinking along the lines discussed in Part 1, then Part 2, which activates it, will be meaningless, or worse, misinterpreted and misused.

Together, the parts constitute a rough sketch, rather than a complete blueprint, for personal achievement in photography. It's your job to finish the sketch your own way. Nobody can do it for you.

JACOB DESCHIN

Thanks for a Helping Hand

To MY WIFE, Celia Spalter Deschin, whose background and training in the science of human relations and whose understanding of what makes people tick, helped me authenticate a merely intuitive faith in the capacity of people to express themselves.

To Paul J. C. Friedlander, whose encouragement, as my editor at *The New York Times*, to express myself freely along progressive lines has afforded me the opportunity to test my conviction that the amateur photographer has far greater potentials for saying things with a camera than is generally supposed, and that these potentials have only to be awakened. The response of readers supported this faith and in consequence inspired the writing of this book.

Thanks, too, to the photographers who were kind enough to let me reproduce their pictures to illustrate and to corroborate the text.

Contents

vii

CONTENTS xi

I saw shapes related to each other. I saw a picture of shapes and underlying that the feeling I had about life.

ALFRED STIEGLITZ

Part 1
Picture Your World

CHAPTER ONE

What's on Your Mind, Photographer?

I find it difficult to believe that there is anyone fully unable to say something about the world which is imaged in his mind and heart.

ANSEL ADAMS

MOST AMATEUR PHOTOGRAPHIC efforts misfire because the photographer lacks the basic philosophy that picture making is a medium through which he can express ideas about people, places, and events he himself knows. As a result, his pictures have scant meaning. He does not fully realize this, either because his thinking on the subject is hazy or incomplete or because it is influenced by someone else's ideas and therefore lacks conviction.

First, find something to *say*. You wouldn't sit down to write a letter without some idea of what you wanted to write about. How, then, can you expect to take a worthwhile picture unless you know what you want to record and, more important, why you want to record it?

Most people work so many hours; play or follow other

activities the rest of the time. They spend their working hours in one environment; their leisure hours, probably, in another. Each environment affects them in some way, and they react, emotionally and mentally, according to their natures and their backgrounds.

Everybody reacts. Feelings and thoughts are not the gift or the prerogative of a few. We all have them, for we would have to live in a vacuum to be entirely free of our surroundings, of the multitudinous incidents and experiences that go on all around us, demanding our attention, provoking our responses. Also, each person responds in a unique way. What is noteworthy to one may be nonsense to another, and each has his reasons. The way each person thinks and feels about his world is the index to his personality, the mark of his individuality.

Since we all have these experiences and feel these responses, why is it that, as photographers, amateurs seldom reveal them in their pictures? What holds them back? The know-how? Simple impressions have been recorded with inexpensive little cameras and no more than box-camera technique.

You don't know what you want to say? Nobody can tell you better than you, yourself. You are afraid to picture what you really see? Afraid of ridicule, of being different? Ashamed of your experiences, your environment, your job, your social status?

Then *give* yourself status. Dare to be individual. Speak your mind photographically. Don't turn away deliberately from the real things and real feelings that you know to empty artificialities. Face your life and its realities. Try to understand them and learn to reveal them through your camera. In that way you will grow, both as a person and as a photographer. One will supplement the other. Your pictures will gain in importance and usefulness the more completely you develop your ability to evaluate subject matter from the viewpoint of a mature personality.

Creativity

Don't let such words as "art" and "creative" scare you. Their meaning is very simple, and the rewards of merit they imply are within the reach of every photographer who is willing to make the effort to earn them. But watch out for misinterpretations of these words, which distort their real meaning and make them much harder to understand and to apply to your own work.

A photograph is said to be a product of "art" when it shows skill and taste, and the photographer is called "creative" when his picture shows that he gave it some thought and imagination. So far, fine. But confusion enters when the same terms with the *same* definitions are illustrated by examples that are completely different in depth of feeling and meaningful values. One picture will make you wonder why the photographer went to so much mechanical trouble to produce a technically perfect print but forgot to say anything in it; the other will show good technique, too, but somehow you don't think of looking for perfection because the story it tells holds all your attention.

I think we are safe in saying, then, that you "create" when you introduce a meaning into your picture that is your own; and that you work in the opposite direction, that is, imitate or at best add nothing, when your picture has no meaning or is similar to a picture made by somebody else. We should not overlook the fact, incidentally, that imitativeness was ingrained in us as part of our school training and that it is not going to be easy to subdue the habit. Nevertheless, we know we must, if real creativity is our goal.

By this definition, anyone can be creative who thinks, feels, and makes some effort to interpret his subject matter imaginatively. Some people may be more creative than others because they perceive more deeply, have a better imagination, or can put down their impressions in photographs with greater clarity. However, it is also true that any person will "see" more or less intensely, relative to a particular experience, on different occasions under different circumstances. The variation will depend on the freshness of his mind and sensibilities at the time, as well as on other factors.

Aaron Siskind, who likes to photograph accidental designs in nature, told me that he once passed a certain rock formation without seeing a thing he could photograph but that when he returned months later, he found the place suddenly "full of images." "As people change," he explained, "their needs alter, too. Life takes on other meanings. They see things differently. That which held neither interest nor significance yesterday may be extremely important for them today. The photographer sometimes reveals these changes in the pictures he makes, which in my case are in the form of discovered symbols."

The point I want to make is that creativity is not some unattainable gift reserved for a small group of the elect. You can be creative, and I can be creative, more so at one time than at another, if we give our imagination full rein and if we try. If we try to get under the surface of things, to understand what they mean, and to say something of real value about the subjects we photograph.

We can be creative if we try to be ourselves, to observe as individuals, confident in our capacities to make mature statements about life in photographs. It is as simple—and as hard —as that.

Being Original

"Originality" is another of those words which, like the word "difference," is frequently misconstrued. The first has been decried as impossible of achievement, because "Everything has been done before, there's nothing new left, so what *can* we do except copy?" and the second has been equally misinterpreted by one of our leading teachers of pictorial techniques. "Everybody is calling for something different these days," he told his class. "In the old days we didn't use figures in landscapes. Today we use figures. That's difference."

Actually, "difference" has the same meaning as "originality," namely, uniqueness of concept, a special way of seeing subject matter—not merely physical difference, which is trivial. Originality is in fact akin to creativity, in the sense that the photographer who possesses it is able to see values in a way which is uniquely his own. The subject can be anything, arranged in any way. The eloquent movement of a hand, the way the light falls, a bold compositional treatment, or a particularly revealing facial expression, any of these may turn a familiar impression into a fresh—and original—idea.

Vitality in Pictures

One of my readers once asked me what I meant by the phrase "vitality in pictures." I had not realized until then that the term might not be self-explanatory to everyone. The question drove home to me again the danger of taking certain words for granted in photographic literature because their meaning, and therefore their application, can be interpreted in different ways by different persons—sometimes harmfully—and to some may mean nothing at all.

Vitality, I thought, is the quality of aliveness in a picture as opposed to the static, or the passive. But is not this the principal goal of the photographer in all his work—to put life into his pictures and so fulfill the camera's chief function: to mirror life? My reader's question astonished me, particularly since he was a teacher of photography. If the import of such a seemingly obvious essential of worthwhile picture making were not readily understood, then photography was in a bad way indeed.

Vitality is the composite of a number of attributes which, together, identify a picture as a living experience vividly portrayed. The term can be used to describe importance in the subject matter and can also refer to the depth of insight shown by the photographic treatment. But unless the second is present, the first can easily be lost. For the quality of vitality is introduced in pictures by the photographer and is, in fact, his responsibility as well as his opportunity. We have only to visit a pictorial salon to realize how much damage an unimaginative photographer without insight can do to vital subject matter.

A portrait can have vitality because the subject has this quality and the photographer has made the most of it; or because the subject has other qualities, such as great sensitivity, which the photographer has reproduced in a vital way, that is, with a truly understanding approach and with great feeling. A photograph of a landscape can have vitality—and so can a water scene or a flower or even a few blades of grass. I have seen pictures of action, which are inherently full of vitality, turned into static records by the mumbo jumbo of pictorial "control" manipulations. It all depends on the way a photographer sees his subject and the way he reproduces what he sees.

If we use Webster's definition of "vitality" as "the power of enduring or continuing," then the word means that "something" in a picture which gives it lasting interest. That is, you can look at such a picture again and again without tiring of it.

Impact

About "impact." The word sounds arty and phony, but only because it has been misused. Once I chatted with Dorothea Lange, famous West Coast documentary photographer, about a certain school whose students are taught "expressive photography."

"They talk and they talk and they talk," she said, "but the result in their pictures is just a squeak."

"What do they talk about?" I asked.

"Impact!"

It can be overdone. Impact is not something you talk about. Your picture has it or not. Impact is present in a picture as the natural result of the vitality discussed above. Vitality and impact are two facets of the same thing. The first is put into a picture by a responsive and competent photographer; the second is the photographer's reward—a pronounced effect upon an appreciative observer.

Impact, therefore, is the chief essential in communicating the content of a picture. But too much preoccupation with it may lead to artificiality. When photographers talk about "zip," "zingo," and "punch" in their pictures, watch out. They may mean only empty sensation—what the advertising photographer calls "shock value," for example. "Never mind trying to say anything in the picture; just hit 'em, make 'em look."

Is that good? Yes, to my mind, if you can look at the picture again afterward and still like it. No, I say, if "shock" is all you get.

Paul Threlfall, who is concerned with impact both as newspaperman and as judge on documentary juries, looks for something to back up impact. "As impact is mentioned as the fore-
most requisite in the judging of a picture," he wrote (in the
symposium of judging standards described in Chapter 19,
"Picking the Winners"), "there is always a possibility that the
subject material will lack interest after considerable study."

Realistic Pictures

Even the term "realistic," which certainly ought to be
clear enough, has been erroneously strapped into a synonym for
"documentary" in its narrow sense (see Chapter 20, "A New
Deal for the Camera Clubs"). That is, it has been made to de-
note a class, or kind, of photography instead of being applied,
as it should be, in the fuller sense defined by Webster: "fidelity
to nature or to real life." What is so "documentary" about
that?

"The term 'documentary' is sometimes applied in a rather
derogatory sense to the type of photography which to me seems
logical," says Berenice Abbott. "To connect the term with only
the 'ash-can school' is so much sheer nonsense. Actually, documentary pictures include every subject in the world—good, bad,
indifferent. I have yet to see a fine photograph which is not a
good document."

Everything you photograph is realistic if it reflects your
impressions of the life around you. Real things are not only
the people, streets, houses, and all the other tangibles that exist
in your world. Things are real too when you infuse reality
into them through a special way of "seeing"—*your* special
way. Thus, you can lend reality to a mood by photographing

it and printing it in such a manner that you make others feel the mood about the way you did. You can add reality of deep significance to a seemingly trivial object, like the detail of an old house, a stick of splintery wood found in an alley, or a cloudscape.

The realistic approach in photography is actually nothing more—or less—than telling the truth, as you understand it, about the subject matter you photograph. Anything less than that is not only unreal but may even be dishonest, as in copying verbatim the ideas of others.

An exhibition of "country landscapes" I once reviewed will provide a case history to demonstrate what I mean by "realistic." The photographer followed the standard pictorial approach of detachment in which the meaning of the photographed material often is secondary to the techniques of composition and printmaking. As a result, the show gave only an inkling of the potentialities of picture making in rural communities.

The amateur photographer, inspired by prints on salon walls, has a tendency to idealize falsely the nature of life in the country—its tempo, sense of values, and atmosphere. He visits a farm or village for a few hours or a weekend, shoots superficial aspects of the rich subject matter he encounters, and comes away satisfied that he has exhausted the possibilities of the place.

Understand Your Subject

The truism that you should know your subject before you shoot applies more strongly in rural photography than in most other cases. The serious photographer will try to see under the surface of things, attempt to understand and interpret intelligently through his camera. Most pictures of this kind fail because the photographer with little or no knowledge of country life evaluates his subjects condescendingly as "primitive." He is apt to glamorize his notions of country life rather than document what he sees.

He shoots snowscapes which say little about the country because he is more intent on textures, shadows, and the arrangement of lines and masses than he is on conveying an idea. He snaps meaningless, pretty pictures of animals with children. He photographs "characters" rather than human beings who live on a farm.

The photographer must realize that the life of the farmer has distinction, intensity, and homely attractiveness; that farmers on their daily rounds are not merely bits of material that fit into a composition but actual human beings. He must try to get into his pictures the flavor of the locale as it is reflected in the daily life of the people and in their houses, stores, farms, activities of work and play.

It is amazing how little of rural community life has been properly recorded, considering the richness of the material offered. The pictures are there—in the farmer's daily routine, the country storekeeper serving his customers, the town meeting, the soda parlor, the once-a-week movie, the country wedding, the Sunday churchgoers, the rural schoolhouse, the weather that you have to live with and cannot escape from to a warm office or steam-heated apartment, the direct relationship between the success or failure of a crop and the fortunes and thinking of an entire community.

But none of these things were in the pictures at the exhibition. Instead, futile generalizations. The photographer had neither sympathy for the lives of country folk nor understanding of the kind of people they were and the kind of world they lived in. His pictures were superficial because they said nothing about the subject; they were unreal because they did not portray the truth. In fact, the truth never did have a chance because the photographer had not bothered to look for it. He was thinking of something else . . . .

Such pictures are not art. They are not creative because they lack feeling, understanding, and imagination. They are not original for, having nothing to say, there is nothing to be original about. With these qualities absent, such pictures have no life to give them meaning, therefore no vitality and certainly no impact. As for their realistic aspects . . . .

CHAPTER TWO

How Much Know-how
Do You Need?

First find something to say and then find something to say it with.

ARNOLD NEWMAN

WANT TO BECOME a photographer? Just press the button, and you're in!

Maybe that sounds like oversimplification, and it is. But let's look at it this way: When you feel very happy, you sing, or you laugh, or you go around giving away cigars. You want *everybody* to know you are happy; so you tell them in these and other ways.

Does it occur to you that singing is an art, that before you can sing properly you have to know how to read musical notes, train your voice, and practice endlessly? Of course not. You are happy, and you sing. Technically, it is bad singing, but you get something off your chest without worrying about musical technicalities.

You have something to say, and you say it—somehow. It's the same with photography. You carry your little box camera

14

around, and suddenly you run across a subject that interests you. You point the camera toward the subject and press the button.

When you see the print, you may find a lot of things wrong with it. Technically, it is bad. But you've got an image —some kind of image. You have your say.

You may have a friend who knows a good deal more than you do about technique and even knows how to make very fine prints. You see pictures in the magazines, in books, and at exhibitions, and they all look better than yours. But when you compare your technically poor print with a lot of these others, you may find that somehow they do not touch you at all. They lack something. You are not quite sure what it is, but you do know they don't mean a thing to you. Maybe, with all its faults, your picture is better.

All *you* know is what you learned from the instruction leaflet that came with the camera—the barest fundamentals of manipulation—but what "comes out" of your camera— good or bad technically—is a record of something *you* felt, understood, and appreciated. *For the time being,* the result is completely satisfactory.

Given a choice of your print and those other pictures you do not like in spite of their perfection, I'll take yours any time.

Photography Is Expression

Here's why. Photography in its purest, basic sense is like any other natural outlet for expression: fundamental, untutored, spontaneous. You use the camera as a third eye, the "recording eye," as an extension of your vision—to catch an expression, an incident, an attitude, etc., that your eyes have seen and your mind and sympathies have evaluated as interesting, exciting, and revealing.

You react spontaneously, impulsively. You want to shout "Look there!" You point your camera, and you press the button. The result is a real picture, in a way a self-portrait. Every picture is a self-portrait—or should be—of the kind of person you are.

What about technique? Of course you need know-how, but that can wait awhile. You need "know-what" first—and more. Know *what*, feel *what*, have some idea of *what*—then aim the camera and press the button.

Say it, say it, speak your mind freely. Technique, the means of disciplining, of directing your statement, will come later. It will come when your needs demand more know-how, when you feel yourself growing creatively mature, when you have more to say than your limited knowledge permits, when you find that what you say—through the pictures you take— is somehow incomplete, the pictures no longer say what you mean, what you see.

When your questions become more frequent and your technical needs more complex, you will *then* be ready for some kind of formal training. By that time, however, you will have become immune to harmful influences, for you will have built up a photographic philosophy of your own. All you will want then is some more know-how. You will know what to do with it.

By that time, too, you will have learned that know-how and know-what go along together, inseparably, and that your desire for more technical knowledge is motivated entirely by the fact that the lack of it keeps you from saying the things you want to say with the maximum of clarity.

The Need for Technical Knowledge

But lest I be misunderstood, let me explain.

The prevailing lack of knowledge among amateur and some professional photographers concerning even basic fundamentals of photographic technique, in the shooting as in the processing phases, poses three questions:

1. Is it possible to take interesting pictures without anything more than ability to manipulate the camera controls and a casual understanding of elementary data picked up at random?

The answer, as I have indicated above, is a positive "yes" for at least three reasons: (1) it has been done frequently by youngsters with box cameras, beginners of all ages and some so-called professionals, especially in the magazine field; (2) because of the camera's ability to record a reasonably acceptable image on film almost by itself, any person with fair perceptiveness can take worthwhile pictures; (3) if a subject makes a strong appeal in itself, even the verbatim record can be effective.

2. Will the acquisition of some mastery of the medium make one a better photographer, and if so, why are so few photographers concerned with making the effort?

The first half of this question answers itself, provided that by "better" one means not technical improvement alone but mastery of technique in the sense of being able to say things in pictures more penetratingly, more clearly, and more forcefully than is possible without such knowledge.

The communication that is only partially articulated when the photographer does not understand either the potentials or the limits of the medium can become a full and powerful statement in the hands of one who has taken the trouble to learn how to draw on the medium for whatever he wants to say about the subjects he photographs.

Satisfaction with half measures, a wide disregard for the standards of the craft, and a disinclination to submit to its disciplines any more than is necessary appear to be the current answer to the second half of the question. Morever, the attitude is encouraged by the existence of a special class of photo-finishers, whose highly skilled processing and printing staffs re-move the burden of technical responsibility from the shoulders of photographers, many of whom—though more or less suc-cessful photojournalists—know little about the process that con-verts their push-button efforts into printable negatives and usable photographs.

3. Is it necessary for a photographer to process his own negatives and make his own prints in order to achieve a result that at least approximates the statement he tried to make when he tripped the camera shutter?

The photojournalist says "no" for several reasons, such as that the picture was made when he pushed the shutter re-lease, so the rest is practically mechanical, or that he exercises control over the results by instructions to the printer. Besides, even in the case of those who have the ability, the photographer says he cannot afford to take the necessary time away from actual shooting. And he is probably right, from this point of view.

The amateur and occasional contributor to publications does have the time and should have the incentive of craft ideals to process his own to the best of his ability, but he is often inclined to ape the photojournalist. In fact, so prevalent is the tendency of today's amateurs to imitate the works and the ways of the photojournalist that amateurism in the real sense of enjoyment of a creative avocation has became almost a rarity.

However, the photographer who is truly concerned about getting the last shade of meaning and feeling into his print will insist on seeing the job through himself. He alone knows exactly how he responded to the subject, and only he can know what points to emphasize through appropriate printing controls and what the total effect should be. To produce photographs that will convey most precisely the reactions he experiences in taking pictures, the photographer must continually improve his technical skills. Since only he can do the job best, he must learn how.

Techniques Are for Expression

But it takes more than just technique to make a good picture. In a famous address by Edward Steichen, at a convention of the Photographic Society of America, the dean of American photography said that he found more true photography in the work of high school students than in the prints hung in some salons. His talk was chiefly an attack on what he called the "time-honored shibboleths of pictorialism" and its preoccupation with techniques rather than meaningful subject matter.

"Today's salons," he said, "are characterized by endless repetition. Photographs follow the same pattern over and over again, leading to inanities. There is much talk about composition, centers of interest, leading lines, and curves. Let's get down to the curve of life, instead. Photograph your country, the humanity that moves about you, the life and meaning of things. Forget the bubble dancers, the eggs rolling off a plate.

"Photography is a folk art comparable to other folk arts, such as dancing or music," he continued. "Photography should be a means of free expression, motivated by the desire to record the significant and interesting aspects of daily life and unhampered by pictorial clichés."

Photographers have indeed become so technical-minded that they are in danger of losing sight of the main goal, which is to use the camera as the means without parallel for conveying the ideas and feelings of the photographer as an ordinary human being. Equipment, accessories, materials, and techniques are only the vehicles for the photographer's observations in terms of graphic images, which he uses in place of other mediums of expression, like writing, music, painting, etc.

Like these others, photography as a craft requires skill and understanding of the medium. But just as music, painting, and writing can be hollow expressions if the heart and the mind of the performer are not in them, so in photography mere technique will produce only trite, useless messages.

Should it not be a lesson to photographers that as the medium grows technologically, imagination seems to be less prevalent? We have more techniques and tools than we know what to do with, literally, yet we keep piling them on, without stopping long enough to learn how to use them properly for expressive ends.

I do not mean to give the impression that we should go back technologically to the horse-and-buggy days. The improvements being made in the tools available to the photographer certainly should help him to perfect and extend his capacity for expression over a much wider range. The only question I have is: Why don't they? Each photographer must give the answer for himself.

The gaiety of these spirited steeds has carried over even into winter in this delightful picture by Izis. Seldom has an inanimate subject evoked such a lively mood as in this happily discovered instance.

The children of the Cree Indian tribe in northern Saskatchewan are like children anywhere, photographer Angelo Lomeo observes here. This unusual shot of the Indian children at tug-of-war proves it.

23

A revealing glimpse into a child's world, as caught by Eugene Tulchin. The picture is wonderfully descriptive both of the child's absorbed expression and the details that spell out the atmosphere of the place.

The encircling arms of the two girls as they wait for the policeman's signal to cross the street here provided Marion Palfi with a moving symbol of the protective instinct as well as of affection and friendship.

Life Magazine's Alfred Eisenstaedt is noted particularly for the human touch he gives to his work, here expressed in the reassuring attitude of the nun at the right as she greets a new pupil at school.

The warmth of the relationship between a boy and his horse is described here by Jacques Lowe in the simplest and most affecting terms. The picture gains strength through the use of a close-up view.

It is time for dinner in Mykonos, Greece, Peter Buckley tells us in
this homely kitchen scene, so richly atmospheric that the observer
is made to feel that he is almost there, too, watching

Hine Sets Example

The example of Lewis W. Hine, who started making pictures at the turn of the century and whose pictures have since become classics, may help to frame the answer.

Although all he had to work with was an old view camera and a little basic knowledge of photography, Hine became master of reporting with the camera. A study of his prints, now the property of the George Eastman House, can teach the photographer of today the much-needed lesson that good pictures depend not on effects as such but on straightforward recording of meaningful subject matter by a sympathetic and understanding photographer.

Hine's work shows that photography is best used as a medium of revelation and interpretation. Because his field was the social scene and his motivation the reporting of social injustice, some photographers may feel his methods are of little interest to them. However, his attitude toward the medium should concern all serious photographers. Hine's pictures represent a broad philosophy of picture making applicable to any photographer, namely, that photographs should be more than technical exercises. To Hine, they became thoughtful statements of worthwhile material which had meaning for him.

Hine did not ignore technique; neither did he worship it. It did not matter to him if some figures in his group pictures were not quite as sharp as others, nor does such a detail detract appreciably from the intensely human quality of the prints when they are viewed today. If the composition in his pictures is not quite according to the rules, the nature of his material and the persuasive influence of his feelings about his subject overshadow these faults.

CHAPTER THREE

You're on Your Own

Photographers must understand that they have to see with their own eyes and not with the eyes of other photographers.

ERWIN BLUMENFELD

"AW, BE YOURSELF!"

You have often heard the remark—spoken kidding-fashion but with a strain of annoyance. Insincerity and a false front are fairly obvious in a person and are rejected as such. But in a photograph the same faking is condoned and even applauded.

Imitativeness is a kind of faking, for it tries to give the impression of original work, thereby hurting no one but the photographer himself, who eventually relaxes into the false assurance that his imitations are really his own creations.

"Imitativeness is the amateur's greatest fault," Erwin Blumenfeld has said. "Too often photographers take pictures only of the matter and in the manner they have seen in the work of some other photographer, instead of discovering ideas for themselves."

Actually, imitativeness is based less on the lack of ideas than on the pressures from all sides to conform to established

30

standards. The desire to think for yourself and to act accordingly is discouraged and penalized by denial of the reward that comes only with conformity: approval by your colleagues.

In photography, many such pressures exist in one circle of workers or another. The virtue of objectivity and the tolerance of other viewpoints than your own are extremely rare. We tend to make evaluations in terms of black and white: "Either you make pictures the way we do, or else . . . ."

The situation once prompted W. Eugene Smith to remark, "Let's not try to bend everyone's will to our own will. Possibly this is a period of confusion in photography whence a clearer idea of its function will arise."

Confusion will be yours indeed unless you realize that you can get nowhere as a photographer until you have the courage to strike out for yourself. Lacking that resolve, you can either throw in your lot with those who inhabit that never-never land of mental and emotional fog called "salon pictorialism," or join the documentarians, at the other extreme, who are not faultless either, because they, too, frequently imitate each other.

Before you decide, let's examine your problem together.

But first, the picture in general. Photography is the flourishing medium that we know it to be principally for one reason: people find in it the answer to their need for some medium of expression. Pressing a button and turning out a picture goes a long way to fulfilling that need.

Photographers have all sorts of backgrounds; they think, feel, react in many different ways; have individual personality traits. Why do they allow themselves to be pushed into a mold, turn out the same kind of pictures as everybody else in their group, lose their identity in a meaningless melting pot of vague generalization?

Specifically, why must *you?*

Why must you borrow a personality when you have one of your own? Do you think yours is not equal to the opportunity? Do you think you are not good enough, that your ideas are not important?

Then think again. Because you're wrong. Every person is important; each person by himself as an individual is important. And you are no exception.

Trust your own reactions. Say what you think; make it a habit to stand on your own feet as a photographer; be yourself. Your rewards will be far more valuable than the ribbons and medals of the salons. You will have a sense of achievement, of pride, of self-esteem and self-importance. And your pictures in consequence will be better—because they will be your very own.

Stieglitz and Originality

One of the most stimulating examples of independent thinking by a photographer is Alfred Stieglitz, whose work teaches us the valuable lesson that the photographer must rely on himself for originality, that he must depend upon his own understanding and inventiveness, free himself from inner doubts of his own worth and from outside compulsions to copy the past and to ape the work of contemporary photographers.

The idea of "originality" gets a good deal of knocking around in all photographic circles. We talk about it but do little to attain it. To Stieglitz, originality was a necessity. He was bored and impatient with the old ways; he had to find new ones, ways that would help him to tell more and to say things better than they had been said photographically before.

By comparison with the richness of photographic materials

and equipment available today, Stieglitz had little to work with, yet he achieved results that seemed impossible to the photographers of his time. He photographed in snow and in rain and outdoors at night. His picture "The Terminal," made during a New York snowfall in 1892, showing the vapor rising from horses hitched to horsecars, has an ingenuity and resourcefulness that are badly lacking in the work of today's amateurs.

The fact that Stieglitz made pictures that were revolutionary for his time, despite the handicap of the then-existing limitations in materials and equipment, is secondary. His example has the greater significance for today's photographers because although he appreciated the importance of technique he did not allow it to enslave him. Rather, he used technique to realize his ideas, never for its own sake.

Believe in Yourself

It takes real personal conviction to do things your own way, especially when yours goes completely counter to the conventional approach. Lack of confidence in himself makes the photographer an easy prey to conformity. Once he gets real ideas, however, the desire to put them across becomes so strong that self-confidence is induced by the sheer pressure of the need to say something. To the point, in fact, where even timid persons find it easier to be "different."

But difference is not enough. The desire to be original may lead even the professional astray. Ezra Stoller, speaking for his fellow architectural photographers, says that some photographers, self-consciously artistic, use dramatic, exaggerated angles to get startling effects under the illusion that they are photographing creatively. It is their business to give something to their picture, but sometimes they go too far, with the result that "too often you can't see the architecture for the picture."

A photographer in another field relies on forced photographic effects to get "eye appeal." In yielding to the temptation, familiar to experimental photographers, to do something different in the belief that difference means, or can make for, originality, this photographer sacrifices conviction and directness.

Limitations

The basic premise of experimental photography is that the so-called "limitations of photography" often lie less in the available techniques than in the vision and imagination of those who use the techniques. Bruce Downes once referred in an editorial in *Popular Photography* to "the continuing struggle to overcome photography's inherent limitations," adding that "photography is a perpetual compromise between what one wants to do and the limitations of both the medium and one's self." Perhaps the key to the problem lies, as Mr. Downes hints, rather in the limitations of photographers themselves than in those of the medium. With all its limitations, which as every working photographer knows, are fewer today than in earlier decades, potentials for creative work still lie well within the bounds and have yet to be fully exhausted.

The tendency to stress the technique's shortcomings puts undue emphasis on what is really only the vehicle for carrying the ideas of whatever a photographer may have to say. Photographers are more limited by inhibitions resulting from conformity to standards and impressions that are not their own, distrust of their personal responses to material, and inability really to see what they are looking at than they are by technical "limitations." When the emphasis is placed on the latter, photographers are more apt to reach for a multiplicity of methods, such as solarization, montage, or double exposure, than to look more thoughtfully and understandingly at the subject.

No manipulated photograph can ever be nearly so convincing and effective as a straight photograph into which the photographer has put his best thought and feeling and carried through his statement with craftsmanship appropriate to his theme. Any attempt to carry the photographic image beyond the direct print becomes an unwarranted invasion of alien mediums. A photograph is a two-dimensional picture in which some effort has been made to give an illusion of what the person, place or thing looked like at a particularly significant moment. A photograph is not a painting, it is not music, nor literature, nor poetry. It can suggest these things, but it would be futile to imitate them (as some have attempted to do through elaborate manipulation). Photography stands alone, unique; limited, it is true, but encompassing worlds of opportunity within its boundaries, as do all the other arts within theirs.

Develop an Original Picture Sense

As an aid in developing an original picture sense, Erwin Blumenfeld suggests that the amateur give himself assignments rather than shoot haphazardly without thought or planning. "You cannot simply walk around with a camera around your neck, hoping that a picture will come along somehow," he says. "The photographer must know what he is after, develop a photographic idea, then go look for it in nature. Give yourself an assignment; choose something to shoot at. From time to time you will come across material that fits in with your theme.

But do not give merely an exact rendering of what you see; look for a personal interpretation and put this in the picture. Create something that was not seen before. The best pictures are those which reveal that the photographer saw something he liked and gave it a personal meaning. True creativeness involves the human spirit."

Practicing what he preaches, Blumenfeld's approach is far from routine. Highly inventive, he sees every assignment as a new problem calling for an individual solution, an opportunity for experiment in the mediums at his command.

Photograms and Exercises

The making of photograms, which are pictures produced without a camera, is often recommended as an exercise for developing creative ability in photography. Joseph Breitenbach, who begins a course in advertising principles by teaching his students how to make photograms, believes the medium is unexcelled for expressing abstract ideas and for training in the imaginative aspects of graphic presentation.

"The photogram has the same relation to photography," he says, "that the abstract form has to painting. It is purely an exercise without meaning, in which the distribution of lights and darks and the movement of lines create a feeling of third dimension.

"The photogram is a medium for seeing realistic objects in an abstract way. It stresses the creative approach and excites the mind to speculation about the third dimension."

A photogram is made by placing an object on photographic paper and exposing the paper to light. The exposed sheet of paper is then developed in the usual way, fixed, and washed. The result is a predominantly black image, where the light has struck the paper without interference. Other portions are white silhouettes and shades of gray, depending on the degree of opacity or translucency of the objects that intercepted the light.

Experimental Photography

Representative in spirit of a growing minority of thoughtful experimental photographers is Vladimir Telberg-von-Teleheim, whose aim is to exploit the known techniques for greater imaginative goals. His purpose is to photograph "not that which is seen but that which goes on in one's mind." To this end, he uses physical objects very much as one may use words, to suggest rather than to depict.

"The pictures should be felt rather than pronounced," he explains, "and an effort to translate them into words may only bring on frustration. My technique is based on the premise that photography need not be just one instant caught and held by the click of a shutter. A conventional photograph of a sunset may be a complete record of the physical factors of the scene as it rests on the retina of the eye. The mind, however, will fuse the sunset with very personal elements, such as the memory of a face, a fireplace, a ship, etc."

His method is that of multiple exposure, either in the camera, when taking the picture, or in the enlarger, when making the print. In the latter case, he projects several negatives, suitably arranged and exposed for a planned result, onto a single sheet of paper, which when developed produces the completed picture. Frequently, he superimposes negative images one over the other.

To give an effect of indistinctness, in a picture he names "A Scream from Long Ago," the brightly illuminated, distorted face of a woman is almost completely out-of-focus. A clearly remembered incident is printed sharply and in full tone; a hazy idea of a tragic experience is conveyed in a darkly printed scene. The deep perspective of a corridor receding into limitless distance suggests "Destination of Memory." A self-portrait, "Preoccupation with the Unsolvable," shows half the face very sharp, the other half out-of-focus.

This reaching out for something beyond ordinary visual experience is a rather bold and extreme instance of the experimenter's efforts to push photography to its limits. Success is rare in such attempts to work out a personal approach—in this case, a combination of photography and psychiatry. Few try to go this far.

Another notable example of joining two mediums to produce a single expression is the work of Wright Morris, whose photographs in his book "The Inhabitants" are more easily understood because word descriptions are introduced. His mediums are photography and literature. No people appear in his pictures, only deserted places, houses, streets. The places are "inhabited" by the memories put into words by the photographer. The words make the places come alive. As in the case of Telberg's pictures, the photographer needs not only ability and understanding in two fields but the extra talent of fusing the two in a single visual communication.

Individual Style

How one photographer achieved a means of introducing a personal element in his picture taking is illustrated in the career

of Art Kane, New York art director and photographer. As
an art student at Cooper Union, he was introduced to photography as part of the curriculum rather than from choice. But the
basic training he received there in the appreciation of design
elements later served to build his photographic style. When,
some time later, he realized the potentials of the camera in recording his impressions, he found that "shapes alone were not
enough to satisfy me; I had to incorporate story telling.

"From then on my approach changed. I was now able to see
things and to stop things within the content of the film frame
in what I felt was an individual manner, my personal reaction.
In an effort to combine story telling and design I found myself
constantly searching for something in addition to the subject
matter itself. My sense of design helped me to create my own
graphic personality, to give an individual interpretation to
everything I find worth photographing."

That he felt the insistence on design might get the better
of his style and end in monotony is indicated by later work
in which Kane puts design aside to concentrate entirely on the
subject itself. Here the photographer's sense of ordinary human
values comes through more clearly and helps the observer
to appreciate the better his stylized efforts. Perhaps the more so
because the design is not calculated but is an inherent part of
the arrangement of the subject as he selects it in his camera
finder.

In Chapter 18, "Lessons at Exhibits," I point out the value
of looking in on print shows as one of the best ways to help
you find your place in photography. I should also like to advise
you to study picture magazines and photographs in other peri-
odicals, such as general-interest and fashion magazines. These
contain some of the best work being done in contemporary

photography and offer a rich source of inspiration for the amateur interested in finding stimulus for developing an individual
style.

A distinctive style is rare in photography. The lack of it
is particularly noticeable among the younger photographers,
many of whom appear to be more concerned with kinds of
material—which incidentally are treated with little variation in
approach—than in developing an individual manner. The result
is a monotonous repetition of statement that, with a refreshing
exception now and then, keeps telling us the same thing over
and over again and in almost the same way. An individual style
in a photographer can actually give new content to a picture
even though the subject itself has been handled many times
before.

"Like the painter," writes Helmut Gernsheim, the British
historian of photography, "the photographer has his individual
style, which is the expression of his judgment, taste, and feeling.
His judgment is evident in the selection of the hour of the day
at which the object or view is shown in the best light. His taste
displays itself in the selection of the most favorable viewpoint;
his feeling is exhibited in the choice of the subject itself. All
this will be immediately apparent to anyone who has seen a
representative selection of a photographer's work."

Individual Style through Diversification

A style is best achieved through experience in photographing a variety of subjects. Amateurs have less need to specialize
in one kind of photography than do professionals, whose
customers, editors, and audience practically oblige them to.
Nevertheless, amateurs often do specialize and thereby miss

opportunities to improve their over-all abilities and sense of values.

No less an authority than Philippe Halsman, noted magazine photographer, recommends variety in photographic experience. A specialist's work tends to become routine unless he looks for inspiration and ideas in other fields, he says.

Although best known as a portrait photographer, Halsman experiments with other subjects whenever he gets the chance, because he believes that activity in several fields helps to make him progressively more effective as a photographer of any one subject. "For example," he explained, in commenting on a group of his dance pictures, "the main problems of dance or stage photographs are the choice of the important moment, the catching of the characteristic expression, and the selection of angle, composition, and lighting, which portray and emphasize the mood of the whole. But these are the problems hidden in almost every picture taken by a photographer. Therefore, these photographs were influence, training, and stimulus for the rest of my work, be it portraiture, fashion, advertising, or reportage."

Diversification is one way to battle conformity. The more kinds of photography you do, the more self-confidence you will gain, and the better you will be prepared to make pictures your own way.

There is an extra advantage in widening your horizon of interests, in looking outside of photography for stimulus. Photographers tend to be chauvinistic, as if the making of pictures were the be-all and end-all of life. Photography is a means of stating your opinions on what you have learned about life. But it should be obvious that your opinions will be worth little unless you take the trouble to find out what life is all about.

Knowledge gives conviction. When you are sure of your ground, nobody can bully you into doing or saying—or photographing—something else. Therefore, get knowledge; and while you're at it, get understanding too, and sympathy. Observe, feel, dig deep. Reach for bedrock until you are satisfied the subject has yielded its essence of meaning and significance for you. When this happens, conformity will have hard sledding. You will know too much—and feel too much—to put up with a fiction and a mask.

You will want to show what you have learned and to show it in the most realistic way you know. And the way will be yours, not one dictated by a cliché.

Nor an imitation, as in one example I recall. An interesting picture of an overhanging ledge of snow brought this comment from a fellow pictorialist: "Where can I find a snow ledge like that?" Obviously, his interest was not in creating his own pictures or in generating his own picture ideas; he wanted to shoot the same subject—and probably in exactly the same way.

Pretty sad? Yes, but more pitiful is the fact that the instance is typical of an attitude of resignation—the inclination and the habit to accept and appropriate the ideas of others because they fit the specifications and because that is the easy way.

Particularly am I concerned about the pure novice in photography, who doesn't belong to the camera clubs, can't tell a pictorialist from a documentarian—and doesn't much care—and who simply wants to shoot pictures. What are his chances for developing an original approach in photography? I should say that his are the best of all, if he can manage to stay away from the influence of the established ideas of any one group long enough to develop opinions and a viewpoint of his own.

Good pictures are not made by rules but by the vision of the photographer, his freshness of imagination, his unique way of looking at and experiencing the world. The best test of a photograph is the feeling of intensity it imparts; for if the photographer has felt strongly about his subject he will succeed in communicating what he felt through his photograph.

BRUCE DOWNES

Part 2
Techniques Are Words

CHAPTER FOUR

"What Shall I Shoot?"

There were two things I wanted to do. I wanted to show the things that had to be corrected. I wanted to show the things that had to be appreciated.

LEWIS W. HINE

BECAUSE LEWIS W. HINE had charted his course as a photographer, he had no trouble finding what to shoot. He knew what he wanted to do. Amateurs will tell me, "Oh well, that was O.K. for Hine. He was one of those 'social-significance' guys. But we want to have fun. We don't want to sell anybody anything."

Go ahead, have fun. But Hine was having fun, too. His was a finer kind of fun than we usually imply by the word. It was the fun that comes from a feeling of satisfaction because you are doing something useful, like communicating your ideas to others through pictures.

Let's see if the word means the same thing to all of us. In photography, we have fun when we shoot wind-blown trees, picturesque old houses, landscapes with winding roads, a cos-

45

tume portrait (which, incidentally, is frequently more a picture of a costume than a portrait).

Is that fun? It *can* be fun if you put something of yourself into the picture and try to reveal an idea about the house, road, etc., that is in some way related to your general thinking, your own honest feelings of what the subject means to you. It *can* be fun if instead of shooting the same old subject over and over and over again in the same old way, as others have done many times before you, you approach it in a personal way. If you try to examine the subject more studiously, try to penetrate its meaning more deeply.

Is that asking too much when all you want to do is have fun? Perhaps you will be able to answer the question better if you compare photography with other interests, like playing a game of cards or engaging in a sport. Certainly a game is fun, but it becomes much less fun when the going is too easy, when your opponent is such a poor player that he offers you practically no resistance, no problem.

There's no fun where there's no fight, no challenge to your own abilities. There's real fun only when your opponent is so good that he keeps you hopping and guessing all the time, when you have to reach way down for all your resources in an effort to outsmart him. *Then* when you beat him, the fun you're having is real and stimulating. It's the fun of solid achievement, by comparison with which the other experience is insipid and boring.

That's the way it is with photography, too, if you'll give photography a chance to prove it. You can take subject matter as it is handed to you—in club assignments, on camera trips, in the various lists of what you should photograph—or you can hunt it up yourself to suit your personality, to fit in with your experience and understanding, and to mirror the things you see and feel.

The fun of photography is in the challenge to your abilities to get the most meaning out of the subjects you photograph —subjects that have personal meaning simply because you choose them yourself, because something in the subject stirs a response in you. Photography is far less fun when you routinize it to fit a bunch of clichés. Like playing a game or sport that is too easy, you take such pictures without enthusiasm and soon lose interest.

Know Yourself First

The very question "What shall I shoot?" is admission of a basic confusion. You ask this question only when you are not quite sure why you own and use a camera. You get into the habit of asking it when you submit to the artificial, unstimulating, and inexpressive goals of salon pictorialists. You ask it when you don't know where you stand as a person.

The camera is a means of "giving out" what you feel and think about anything that interests you. You can neither feel nor think coherently unless you have some over-all idea of your relationship to the things around you, of their meaning for you as a sympathetic and intelligently responsive human being. (I use the term "intelligence" in its real sense of native understanding rather than the result of formal education. Intelligence is something you have; education is something you get.)

Such an outlook will give your thinking direction, purpose, and clarity. Subject matter will then be a very personal factor. You will realize that nobody can really tell you what to shoot.

That is your job. You move about a given locale, and certain things catch your attention for certain reasons—maybe a surface or a design, a face, a gesture, or an incident. When the subject hits you hard enough, you take a picture.

Photographers who have difficulty in finding subjects often do not know what they are looking for. They shoot indiscriminately because they don't take the trouble to clarify things for themselves. They have no viewpoint, no philosophical base of operations to help them shape, then sharpen, their reactions.

Isn't it a common human experience that when somebody tells you to do something you get far less satisfaction from doing it than when you think of the idea yourself? You get a kick out of the notion that the idea is your own. In photography, we have a real opportunity to exploit this vanity to the full and at the same time achieve not only the thrill of discovery but also the deep inner triumph and release of a vital expression.

Instead, we frequently take the easy way: "Let someone else do it." That is where the subject suppliers take over and shove the amateurs still deeper into the lethargic position of a button pusher doing another's bidding. The more you avoid doing your own thinking, the weaker becomes your capacity to think when you ultimately decide to kick over the traces of conformity and to go your own way.

The Thematic Approach

To the perennial question, "What shall I photograph?" Dorothea Lange's answer is, "Pick a theme and work it to exhaustion; then pick another, or handle several themes at a time.

"So many people handling a camera come to a place where they don't know what to do next," says this noted West Coast photographer and member of the famous Farm Security Administration group. "If they were to choose a theme instead of taking pictures haphazardly, they would soon find they have plenty of material to shoot at. It is important, however, to work freely, not from a shooting script but in spontaneous response to whatever comes along that fits the theme or themes the photographer is working on. Let yourself loose on a theme; it is the only way to make the most of it."

Miss Lange counsels amateurs to be receptive to new discoveries—". . . not much sense in photographing what you already know." Picture taking should be a strictly personal undertaking if it is to give the greatest satisfaction to the photographer. He should choose themes about which he feels the most keenly, then try to exhaust his efforts in following them through. No theme is ever really finished, she says; there comes a time when the photographer feels he has nothing more to say on the subject; at least for the time being. There will be days when he will see nothing in the subject, other days ". . . when everything you see will fall into place.

"The secret is attention—observation and receptivity. Moreover, you have to know what you are going to do with the pictures afterward. Since pictures are a medium of communication, the photographer should have some use goal in mind. I truly believe that if you follow a subject or undertaking far enough there will be a place for it somewhere. A prime requisite for success is that the subject be something that you truly love or truly hate."

Edward B. Kaminski, Los Angeles teacher of photography, believes that amateur photographers tend to hedge themselves in with technical and mental restrictions and hesitate to express themselves individually, preferring to be told what to do in photography rather than to work spontaneously to satisfy personal needs.

"We have a fear of being different," he says, "a fear of being ourselves. We don't like to be left out; we want to conform. Most people do not know what to shoot and so are content to take the easy road and accept club assignments that usually have little meaning for them personally. We might take a lesson from the child of, say, one to five years of age. The child does not have to be told what to be interested in. He is just naturally interested, vitally so, in every detail of his environment. It is in his nature to be excitedly curious about everything. And so it is with the truly creative photographer.

"Individual betterment in photography comes only with the development of confidence in one's own ideas and enough assurance to present them, no matter how they may run counter to conventional results," he says. The subject itself is not important, only how the photographer feels about it.

Working by Yourself

Photography is an individual pursuit. You work best and most productively alone. When gregariousness is introduced, photography suffers. Either your pictures have little meaning, or—equally bad—they are similar to the ones made by other photographers.

Gregariousness in photography is promoted and exploited by the subject suppliers: the camera trips under some leader's guidance, the camera-club "studio nights," the lighting demonstrations at photographic shows arranged to give amateurs subject matter to shoot at. The last two exercises could be made constructive if they were presented merely on the basis of in-

struction in the principles of lighting. But the impression is
that actual subject matter is being offered, with the result that
pictures taken on such occasions are often submitted in contests and sent to exhibitions as the work of the photographer—
even though the lighting and posing ideas, if any, are the work
of the demonstrator or lecturer.

Equally misleading, and in a way harmful to the amateur
photographer, are most camera trips. These are excursions to
near or distant places, by car, train, ship or even airplane, for
the purpose of taking pictures under the leadership of a guide,
whose function is to help you find pictures and give you
technical advice. As if photography were like fishing, shooting game, or picking berries! All you have to do is to get
there; the subjects are just waiting to be picked off.

The camera trip is a contributing factor in the growing
distortion of the function of photography—or our ideas of it.
The facts are completely ignored: that photography is a personal matter, that you don't take pictures in droves but all
by yourself, that picture taking must be done reflectively, and
that reflection is a lonely business.

Study Your Park

Take Central Park in New York City. There are Central
Parks everywhere, of course, but I'm going to discuss this one
because I live in New York and, therefore, know it best. You
can't find a more suitable place for reflection, but you would
never know that from some of the salon pictorials the park
has yielded.

Central Park is more than merely the outdoor studio for
snapshots of relatives and friends that it seems to have become

over the years. New York's "big front yard" offers possibilities for really fine pictures, but it probably yields fewer good ones than any other part of the town.

That may be partly because most photographers take the Park for granted without bothering to investigate imaginatively its many significant features. They shoot pictures thoughtlessly, attracted largely by the cavortings of ducks, squirrels, pigeons, and the zoo animals, or by pointless compositions and confused masses of foliage.

Central Park has connotations that go deeper than its surface attraction. It is much more important to understand these values and to photograph them intelligently and interpretively than to know which film or filter to use. The techniques are universally applicable, whether in Central Park or elsewhere.

First, the Park must be recognized for what it is and what it means to the people who go there. One might call the Park a sort of wilderness, spacious and free, where people go to escape the tensions, worries, and annoyances of the big town. Humanity comes to the Park to relax, to play, to think in its unhurried atmosphere.

As you pursue this thought, the Park acquires a new meaning, and picture subjects suggest themselves on every hand. The rock formations and land elevations become more than physical irregularities, on which people sit or climb. They become sanctuaries for the lonely. Notice how many people like to sit on high rocks to read or to sun themselves or perhaps to escape from the monotony and regularity of the city streets.

One convenient approach is to line up a few subjects and, taking one at a time, explore its possibilities. The Park has lakes, bridges, bridle paths, statues. It has cement pavements fissured by time. It has grace, movement, and space. Relate all these to people and to their need for an occasional return to simplicity.

Lighting helps to tell a story effectively; point of view strengthens it; and people give the picture the value of a sympathetic human document. The best pictures will be candid. Posed pictures almost always give themselves away and seldom ring true. The photographer has to watch his chances, work unobtrusively, and shoot quickly. Children, who are more natural in the Park than elsewhere, make excellent subjects. Animal and bird life can be put in touch with human life under favorable circumstances.

Statues and trees can be related to people. The sweep of line of a bridge, a winding path, or lake shore can frequently be used to express the character of the Park. The important thing is that you get the "feel" of the Park. Once you have that, subjects will not be hard to find. They will crowd in on you faster than you can photograph them. It's that kind of place. Like your own Central Park too, maybe, wherever you may live.

Subjects by Imitation

When photographers find themselves at a standstill as responsive human beings, they look for scapegoats to justify their reluctance to think. Subject matter then becomes something that they pick because it fits a formula or has been done by someone else. They fall back on pictures they recall, on the clichés of the salons, on cribbing from a fellow photographer by taking the same picture he is taking.

The last case is particularly common among amateur groups. They will go off in threes or fours or more because they are afraid to stand by themselves, too lazy to work things out alone. Because they lack self-confidence and have been taught to follow certain fixed patterns of thought, they are bored and unhappy until they recognize in a subject the elements of an accepted pattern. Once these are discovered by any one of the group, the others crowd in to take the same, or a very similar, picture.

It would be funny if it were not such a sad commentary on the waste of the creative faculty inherent to some degree in everybody. Worse than the fact that they are all shooting the same thing is their failure to realize that they are imitating and that imitativeness actually retards development of whatever creative capacities they may possess.

This poverty of imagination and the desperation that results reaches its final humiliating phase in the club competitions, when the photographers bargain among themselves to determine whose picture should be entered. Arguments develop over questions of priority (who saw the subject first?) and point scorings (who needs the points more?). The picture becomes a piece of merchandise instead of a personal expression. While photographers haggle over the price, creativity is sold down the river.

Another scapegoat for the nonthinking photographer is the matter of equipment. Too bad that much repetition has outworn the old truism—more true today than ever before because of the confusing and distracting avalanche of equipment available—that it's the man behind the camera who counts. We keep forgetting. It is said that no one has yet exhausted the potentials of the ordinary box camera.

Instead of looking at his world with a searching mind and attempting to crystallize a few things for himself as well as for others, the photographer too often turns on his camera and yearns for that new gadget, blaming his equipment for the lacks in his personality. Maybe that new-type camera with the squidget on it will help him to make better pictures, or maybe he needs a red filter or that new this-and-that.

It seldom occurs to him that maybe what he really could use is a new-type viewpoint, a reappraisal of his function as a photographer, a dusting off of the cobwebs so that he can find his real self at last, learn his real needs as a photographer: to say something and to say it as well as he can with the techniques at his command and the equipment he now owns.

"What shall I shoot?" will then be no problem. Instead, the problem becomes "How can I say it with enough clarity and conviction so that others will understand what I have shot?"

CHAPTER FIVE

You Have to Like People

I want to give the human feeling.

ANDRÉ KERTESZ

WHEN YOU GET too far away from people, you lose the human touch essential to the finest opportunities photography has to offer. I don't mean you have to keep photographing people all the time and nothing else. Pictures have been made in which there is not a sign of a person, yet the effect is such that you feel the subject is related to people. They have a human atmosphere.

Wright Morris, in "The Inhabitants" (see Chapter 3, "You're on Your Own"), filled a book with pictures that contain no people yet have such a marked human quality that you feel people must be around somewhere. The pictures are the homely signs of ordinary living: a barn, an old rowboat tied to shore, a doorway, a lonely street, a porch, a stoop, the steps back of the house—and houses, houses, houses, worn old places that people have lived in, people like you and me. There are no people in any of the pictures, yet the pictures seem to be full of people.

On the other hand, I have seen pictures of people that are

56

not people at all. Real people, that is. They are something the photographer dreamed up to resemble people, to give people attributes they do not have. I refer to some of the salon concoctions, in which a person is used to symbolize a theme of some sort, an inhuman ideal like "Love *Was* a Dove"—or something—in which, as you may have guessed, the model is a female nude.

Maybe I should not mention the subject, since nude "studies" by amateur photographers are a pet aversion of mine. Not only are they totally meaningless, but in most cases the photographer's motivation is questionable. Insincerity and the lack of a genuine idea are betrayed by the very titles the pictures are given, like "Despair" and "Abandon," describing poses that in most cases are unbelievably silly. Such pictures are neither real nor imaginative. They are the worst examples of the amateur's proclivity for imitating—this time, the artists.

In a somewhat milder form, but equally obnoxious in motivation and useless to photographers, is the cliché of the model-in-bathing-suit offered as "subject matter" at various commercial photographic shows and demonstrations. Its only value is to "bring in the customers"; its effect is to lower the reputation of photography in the eyes of the general public and to make many of the photographers themselves slightly ashamed of their hobby.

Pictures Tell about People

In contrast are the realistic pictures by Leonard McCombe, one of *Life*'s top photographers. He says he makes pictures to entertain or inform people about people. People see themselves mirrored in the behavior of others, and when such records are done with this expert's skill, the pictures do inform and do entertain.

Pictures of people should "talk," tell stories, provoke thought, and help understanding without the aid of captions, McCombe believes. The photographer should make his pictures come alive so vividly that the subject seems to be talking to the observer, telling him how happy or how sad he feels, what he is thinking.

McCombe knows what he wants, and he goes after it. He throws himself into his task so enthusiastically that he becomes identified with his subject matter, much as an actor identifies himself with his role. As a result, he gets to know his subject so well that his pictures never fail to say something important about the person's character.

McCombe uses a miniature camera exclusively because it gives him the freedom of movement and flexibility of camera position demanded by the fleeting nature of his subject matter —people. A gesture or facial expression must be caught in an instant, or it will lose its spontaneity and naturalness.

The photographic approach to people varies with the personality of the photographer. Some give themselves away almost every time they take a picture; something of the photographer shows up to reveal him for what he is.

Two Photographers

Cases in point are two photographers I know. The pictures of the first are deliberate, studied, almost arranged, but warm with understanding. Though belonging roughly in the candid class, they appear posed and camera-conscious. Nevertheless, his subjects are not really camera-conscious, in the static sense, but appear to be merely curious and absorbed. It is as if the photographer had suddenly asked his subjects to stop whatever they were doing, please, and sit for his camera. This photographer is curious; he is interested in the subtle characteristics of people rather than in the more obvious traits that the candid style reveals.

He likes people, and because he likes them, he tries to penetrate a face to the personality that lies beneath. The more he "digs," the more he shows up himself. The personalities that he reveals are a composite of the personality that *he* is. Because he is looking for reflections of himself, he photographs only those people—men, women, children—in whom he senses little bits of himself.

The second photographer is more or less objective; he seems to prefer generalizations about people and their environment. His pictures describe people as groups and how they look and act against the background of the places in which they live. He does not like to get too close to people. He prefers the broad idea rather than the specific—universal meanings and the guiding forces of atmosphere and the nature of the locale.

The first photographer likes to pin things down in terms of individuals, one at a time or in small groups, close up; the other, to make personal statements about people in general.

You may prefer one or the other approach, but it is not a question of which is the better viewpoint. Both are good, both interpretive, stimulating, and informative. Most important is the fact that both men express themselves in personal ways, making clear what they are trying to say without flourish or attitude. Both reveal a sincere attempt to understand and to make honest comments in their pictures—and in making these comments, to tell us something about themselves as well.

Know People

The photographer Arnold Newman speaks for all honest photographers when he says that his aim is "just to show what people look like and to show as much about them as possible."

To show what people look like, you have to get to know about them. That takes curiosity about the things that concern them and the influences that make them what they are. You cannot have this curiosity unless you like people, nor can you get to understand people unless you are sympathetic toward humanity in general.

You may even wish to photograph persons whom you do not like, in order to get across some of the things you believe to be bad. But that will be because you care about people generally and about what happens to them. You can photograph "bad" persons by catching expressions or gestures that emphasize their badness. In that way, you can also show that people have evil aspects, like selfishness and callousness. Or you may wish to show how these aspects can be harmful to the welfare of people in general.

"Candid" documentary photographers often take pictures of this kind, but amateur photographers in the main prefer to take pictures of people whom they like and simply avoid those they don't.

Some photographers tell me that they never take pictures of people or of subject matter in which people appear. This may be due to a kind of shyness. Or maybe they are just too lazy to tackle the extra technical problems involved when people are included in a scene. It seems to me, though, that if you leave people out of pictures *only* because you do not like to include them, since you have no feeling for people, then all your pictures must in consequence have a lifeless quality.

Objects and places take on significance chiefly because you associate people with them. Things are what they are because of people; because of people, they have warmth and meaning and photographic interest. A brand-new house that has never been lived in is not nearly so photogenic as a worn old house that has been occupied for years. (Pictorialist and documentarian both know that and make the most of it—though each in his own way.)

To return to Newman's quotation: What I think he means by wanting to "show as much about [people] as possible," is that a close-up, or "head shot," of a person does not always tell the whole story. Sometimes we need to include some of the background, the environment in which the person lives. Newman does a good deal of professional portraiture, in practically all of which he includes objects that help to describe the person's character. In one extreme case, the portrait of a famous pianist, he devoted most of the picture space to the piano, the image of the subject himself occupying a small space in a corner of the picture. Newman felt that in giving this emphasis to the piano, the pattern of which, incidentally, suggested a musical note, he described his subject in the best way he knew.

When he showed this picture during a lecture, he was severely criticized. "Newman is not interested in the people before the camera," said his critic. "He has a tendency to become interested more in the background than in the man."

However that may be, it is Newman's way. Although to some people the place of environment in his pictures of people may appear exaggerated, his basic premise that photographers should not stint on backgrounds to the extent they do certainly deserves consideration. We are too prone to take conventional portraits instead of trying to get a more complete impression of the person by including something extra, a supporting detail or two to help describe the subject better and to bring out an important facet of his personality or profession.

Supporting Details in Portraiture

Perhaps one reason photographers do not use background material as much as they should is the fact that technical and artistic problems are thus introduced which many photographers are unable or unwilling to cope with. It's much easier to "compose" a close-up portrait than it is to relate the subject to a background. However, this is a weak excuse and may be promptly rejected in the face of the opportunities offered to tell a more revealing story.

A picture that includes some aspects of the subject's environment helps us to understand him better. We relate the objects to the man and thus fill out the interpretation the photographer tried to get across in taking the picture. The background makes the subject "come alive," assume a three-dimensional entity.

Of course, the background will have no value if it is not authentic. If the background is introduced for the sake of the portrait, for example, but has no other relation to the environment in which the subject lives, then it is worthless, particularly when it is used to supply a substitute, more flattering impression of the subject than would be induced by the real thing. In these circumstances, the portrait degenerates into a masquerade, a rather common occurrence with portrait "studies" hung in pictorial salons.

One instance will suffice to illustrate the kind of thinking that goes into the making of such pictures. One of our promi-

nent pictorialists, who has been winning honors in salon competitions over a number of years, has a penchant for Bowery
bums—especially Bowery bums with blue eyes. Blue eyes
photograph well, you know.

He found one. But did he photograph him as a Bowery
bum, in the Bowery, an habitué of the flophouses, a beggar?
Don't be silly. How could you hang a picture like that in the
salons? Got to floss things up a bit. Our pictorialist really went
to town. By the magic of soap and water, cleaned-up clothes,
a brand-new corncob pipe, a studied pose, and a 45-degree
light carefully set up in the club studio, our Bowery bum with
the blue eyes was transformed into a respectable—though somewhat tattered—citizen of the realm. The resulting print—size
16 by 20 inches, ferricyanided, beautifully enlarged, brown-
toned, and suitably mounted—subsequently enjoyed much success in the salons. I must admit, it was one of the best camouflage jobs I have seen. But what a monstrous lie!

So there you have it. Motivation—blue eyes that photograph well. And prize ribbons—the bright goal. But meaning
—nil. Feeling, understanding, interpretation—all nil. And the
pity of it is that our pictorialist really *has* capacity for feeling
and understanding and *could* put meaning and interpretation
into pictures—if he had not been the victim for too long of
"salon poisoning."

Human Interest

Totally different is the viewpoint of photographers who
search the highways and byways for human-interest material.
Public events, like parades, are field days for their cameras. The
people who watch a parade usually offer more interesting pos-

sibilities than the parade itself. Much of the latter is routine, little different from other parades and with few ideas to tempt the amateur's camera. However, by combining the watchers and the parade in story-telling incidents, the photographer may relate the two and thus obtain unusual candid pictures that reveal the spirit of the parade and show people's varied reactions.

People are real; photograph them realistically. Avoid "character" studies. Find out about people so that your pictures of them can be authentic, therefore convincing. Don't introduce ideas about them, even for "effect," that do not describe the kind of people they are. Use the ideas that suggest themselves to you as the result of studying their personalities and environment. Your best approach in photographing people is to watch for and learn to recognize aspects of expression, gesture, and attitude that tell you things about them, thus helping you to make pictures that reveal their true character.

The 35mm Way

What is the influence of the type of camera a photographer uses on the kind of pictures he takes with it? Even on a surface appraisal, one may say that the widely prevailing use of the miniature and the characteristic results achieved should amply answer this question. If so, then what about the frequently cited argument that candid, slice-of-life, split-second and similar attitudes usually associated with the miniature can be handled with larger cameras too?

This sounds valid; after all, is it not true that it is the photographer, not the camera, who is candid, or whatever his approach may be? But the big flaw here is that while big-camera photographers, given favorable circumstances, can take the miniature-camera type of pictures, they hardly ever do, and the evidence is plentiful.

However their standards and achievements may differ in quality of vision, photographers using small cameras, and it is obvious that they are far in the majority today, work in similar ways, take almost the same kinds of pictures and are motivated by fairly identical goals. This of course is the general approach, the one most noticeable, not only in this country but in other countries as well.

The casual manner encouraged by the compactness, small size, generous film loading, and great maneuverability of the miniature is a temptation too difficult to resist, especially when one has so many colleagues doing the same thing. The result is enormous multiplication of impressions that seldom can be distinguished from each other. So much so in fact that one leading observer of the scene was moved recently to comment that if one were to shuffle the work of the three or four hundred photographers he sees in the course of a year, it would be a discouraging task to attempt to tell their work apart.

Emphasis on the Human Scene

The current vogue of available-light photography is not of itself the core of the impasse. The constant emphasis on the human aspects of the photographer's world almost to the exclusion of the environment itself, its structures, surfaces, details, and its various natural endowments, has made for a monotony of photographic output. The way people walk, talk, stand, and gesture, the comic and the ludicrous, the gay and the somber moments in man's experience, all have been recorded so often and in so many ways that there seems hardly anything left to say. Of course there is—for photographers with a fresh outlook. But there is much, much more than human material only, and most of it is being missed or overlooked.

The miniature makes easy but does not dictate the kinds of pictures that can be taken with it. It simply frees the photographer to move about without the restrictions of the larger camera. It offers him a veritable arsenal of tools and techniques with which to photograph anything he pleases. Why, then, does he generally insist on closing off his potentials by neglecting to show life in all its aspects rather than the limitations which he has imposed upon himself?

Haphazard Shooting?

Perhaps the reason is the lack of discipline, the inclination to shoot quickly and often in the hope of getting something worthwhile without going to too much effort in the process. Is this the influence of the miniature on today's photographers? Unfortunately, for too many, it is. But for those who can face the challenge of the medium and exploit its wonderful devices, the miniature has been a means of releasing unsuspected reservoirs of expression and communication and of providing the unique facility of a picture-taking vehicle without parallel.

The miniature is popular and becoming ever more so. Predictions are freely made that it will become even smaller, and that the day of the larger camera is doomed. This is undoubtedly an exaggeration for, however optimistic one may be about the small camera's future, the larger one, with its many controls in terms of perspective and angle, is bound to survive in many important applications.

Moreover, it must be recognized that, whatever influence the small camera may have on others, it is almost completely lost on many of those whose temperament demands the deliberate study and subject appraisal that works to best advantage on the ground glass of the view or similar large camera.

CHAPTER SIX

Have Something to Say

*The documentary photographer aims his camera
at the real world to record truthfulness. At the
same time, he must strive for form, to devise effective ways of organizing and using the material.
For content and form are interrelated.*

PAUL STRAND

THE TROUBLE WITH most amateur photographers is that the
lack of something to say does not hinder them in the least.
They photograph anyway, then wonder why the results are
so disappointing. They substitute technical exercises for story
value and personal expressiveness and salve their consciences
with "good print quality."

Why not do the job right, combine technique with meaningful subject matter? Photography has limitless potentialities
for every person who handles a camera. What these potentialities are every photographer can begin to discover for himself if he will do three things:

1. Understand the subject.

What does it mean to him? Why does he want to photograph it? If he cannot answer these questions to him-

self, with some degree of conviction, he will shoot aimlessly, will be confused about what techniques to use, and his picture, as a result, will be pointless.

2. Decide what he wants to show in his picture in order to get across a specific idea.

What does he think and feel about the subject? What comment is he trying to make about it? Does he want to show the idea of elegance, dignity, sympathy, graceful movement, joy, sadness, describe a feeling of drama or romance, depict an atmosphere of calm or one of great excitement? Does he wish to express limitation or great space, the strong light of a midsummer noon or the soft light of an autumn afternoon?

3. Select thoughtfully the techniques necessary to achieve his intention most effectively.

These three—understanding, intention, and technique— are in fact inseparable and should proceed simultaneously in the mind of the creative photographer.

Meaning and Technique

I think most people will agree that technical knowledge is necessary to tell a complete story in a photograph. But technical knowledge alone will not put meaning into a picture where there is none to begin with. Without intelligent and purposeful direction, technique, no matter how well executed, is a hollow triumph. A beautifully graduated study in the gray scale would achieve the same result.

The most common fault of the amateur is that he fails to think through the picture, to approach the subject matter with some attempt to understand it and what he is trying to make it say. He lacks the true understanding of photographic technique, which is that it should be used to report and interpret subject matter from the broad base of a personal philosophy about the world he lives in and his place in it.

What do we mean by "something to say"?

Having something to say presupposes knowledge and understanding of the subject photographed. That is, you have to know what it means to you, at a particular time and in a given place. By "knowledge," I do not mean that you have to know architectural principles, for example, in order to appreciate the beauty of a public building or the charm of a country dwelling. That kind of knowledge is needed in commercial photography, where you must be concerned with certain details for the sake of a record. For an amateur interested in conveying impressions and ideas, *exact* knowledge is not necessarily a prerequisite for taking pictures of a subject.

Instead, the building you are photographing will be related in your mind to the kind of persons who live or work there, the significance of the building in the environment. By aiming your camera from different viewpoints, by waiting for the sun to get around to the right angle relative to the building, and by using other appropriate techniques, you can make the structure look dignified, graceful, somber, or produce any other impression you feel it calls for.

Before you can take a picture you should, therefore, know the nature of the subject, then try to understand its significance. Use the three points mentioned above as a base for your thinking. When you have decided what it is you want to get across in your picture, work out the technical details and make your photograph accordingly. All these steps may take hours or minutes or perhaps only a split second. The more experience you get in recognition of significant subject matter and in the use of techniques, the sharper will be your perceptions, and the quicker you will be able to decide on what it takes to get the picture you want.

Meanings Vary with Time

Subject meanings will differ for you at different stages in your personal development. As life experiences develop various facets of your personality, you will "see" more and with greater depth of appreciation. As you grow, subjects that interested you early in your career may become meaningless, and other subjects will assume an importance they never had before. By the same token, you will interpret *all* subjects from the viewpoint of a richer maturity.

It is this aspect above all that makes photography the fascinating medium that it is, that it *can* be for all photographers who take the trouble to use their cameras creatively.

The *same* subject can also have a different meaning in one locale or circumstance than in another. Flowers, for example. A bed of roses in a rich man's garden may be beautiful, but its beauty may be dignified, detached, and cold. "Very nice," you say, but it does not touch you. A rose from that garden in your lady's hair may stir warmer emotions in you. On the other hand, a rose in the buttonhole of an uncouth person may give a strong feeling of incongruity, perhaps even one of revulsion—or wondering.

A group of roses in a vase on a sunlit window sill in your home will affect you differently. Roses in a broken flowerpot on the window sill of a poor man's home will mean something else again. The beauty and richness of the flowers against the

background of poverty and squalor may move you to philosophical contemplation.

Perhaps we can use these examples to help define what we
mean by "knowledge" and "understanding." Unless we recognize, on the basis of our life experience, that while a rose may
"smell as sweet," it will not mean the same thing in one circumstance as in another, our knowledge is inadequate for full
expression. A child may not see a difference, but an adult should,
because life's experiences should have taught him that differences
exist and that these differences vary his response in each case.

Physical identification of an object is not full knowledge
of it. Maturity develops more complete knowledge, which, in
consequence of the individual's growth, should bring understanding, or appreciation, of the significance of the object. You
understand because you know—in the deeper sense. Because
you understand, you can interpret what you see, show in your
photograph how you feel about it, what you think.

Amateurs have this fault in common: that they tend to
photograph an objective *thing* rather than their ideas about it
—why the thing exists, how it relates to other things, what they
mean to each other and to the photographer, and the part the
thing plays in life's total scheme.

Understanding of a subject is usually followed by the wish
to say something about it. The something you intend to say is
related not only to understanding but also to the techniques
required to make your statement clear.

Unity of Expression

We must recognize these three—understanding, intention,
and technique—as the components of unity of expression. Be-

fore you can achieve this unity, you may have to take one at a time. My thesis in this book is that having something to say should be the principal motivation in creative photography. First you try to understand—yourself, your world; *then* you decide what you want to say about it, that is, give an opinion, put down a reaction.

You can do this with the minimum of technique, as I indicated in Chapter 2, "How Much Know-how Do You Need?" The resulting statement may not be complete—because you lack the required know-how—but it will be a start. You may even find yourself so anxious to get things off your mind that you will not notice, or will ignore, your lacks in techniques. This may be very good in your case. Like dashing off notes to people about things that are happening to you and that you just cannot wait to tell somebody.

How long you will continue in this stage will depend on such personal factors as the patience you have to learn and how eager you are to be clearly understood. Every photographer will view the matter differently. Some will linger at the second phase longer than others.

You can stay longer at this point and still manage to make yourself clear in pictures, provided you relate your expression to the technical know-how you have to date. Keep within the bounds of your knowledge if you wish to be effective.

How much technique you need will depend on the type of subject matter you are involved in at any given time. Many photographers have put their ideas across successfully with the simplest techniques. Your guiding thought should be to have enough technique to say what you want to say well. Do not learn technique merely for its own sake.

At some stage, however, every photographer worth his salt

realizes at last that a complete statement is not possible without a mastery of the needed techniques.

That is when you begin adding to what you know. When you find that you do not have the technique necessary for a given expression, start hunting. If it is not available from others, make some experiments and learn the harder way.

Learning Techniques

You may reach a period, in fact, when a multiplicity of problems makes you very conscious of technique and you wish to concentrate on it alone, without concerning yourself about the first two elements (understanding and intention). This decision may be safely undertaken as soon as experience has taught you that technique alone is pointless; a photographer must have something to say.

Technique can be learned, as much technique as you need. For some the work is uphill all the way; others pick it up more easily. Natural ability is a helpful factor, but the lack of such ability is not a serious bar to progress. The job will simply be harder and take longer. But if you want the goal badly enough, the work will not seem difficult.

The conquest of complicated technique sometimes results in a boomerang: the photographer becomes so enamored of know-how that he overestimates its importance in the scheme of things. This is happening all the time in salons, where the worship of technique has had the effect of beating down the natural impulse of people toward self-expression and of substituting values that have little or no relation to life.

This will not happen to you once you have realized that in order to photograph creatively, you must live creatively, take your part in the stream of life; that technique, even at the peak of perfection, is still only a channel for your thoughts and feelings, not an entity. It will not happen to you if you really have something to say and you really want to say it.

Communication

A picture should be a stimulating experience both for the photographer and for those who see his work afterward. What the photographer selects for treatment is not always so important as what he does with it. The picture's effectiveness will depend on the photographer's success in drawing from whatever the material happens to be some aspect of it that he has seen freshly and produced with enough skill to evoke a similar response from the observer of the finished print.

The more simple the material, the greater, on the whole, is the demand on the photographer's craftsmanship. Simplicity is deceptive; the object as object may give no sign of its potentialities photographically except to those who can see beyond the surface values. Such ability on the part of the photographer comes naturally with some, the rare few. With most persons, it can be developed to some degree through training in observation. Along with this quality must grow the faculty of recognizing and being impressed by some distinctive feature either indicated or suggested by the object.

However, for the photographer as for those who use other graphic mediums, responsiveness and even understanding, vital as these are, can find expression only through a mastery of the medium. Inadequacy in this respect can void the most sensitive idea; one must know how to describe photographically what one has to say about anything. The less craftsmanship, the more limited the capacity of the photographer to reveal his discoveries in reasonably communicable terms.

CHAPTER SEVEN

Say What You Mean

I know what *t' say; it's the sayin' o' it.*

J. M. BARRIE'S "THE LITTLE MINISTER"

"THAT'S THE WAY I WANTED IT."

You know the type. Painters know him too. And the exasperating thing about the remark is that you cannot argue with it. It is the perfect rebuttal. After all, a man does have a right to make a picture the way he wants it.

On the other hand, one cannot be blamed for interpreting the remark as a smoke screen for a badly made picture or an attempt to be "arty" in order to give the impression of originality and imagination. This is what happens when a photographer pretends to have more technique than he has. He hurts only himself—by retarding his progress through disinclination to recognize his failings and to do something constructive about them. He impresses few, if any, because sham is fairly transparent.

Say what you mean, certainly, but have something meaningful to say, and say it so that it can be understood.

Somewhat in the same vein, when a photographer is asked to select his best pictures, he often picks out nearly his worst.

76

At least, others do not agree with his choice as representative of his best work and in many cases actually dislike the pictures altogether.

Does the photographer have a dulled critical sense where his own pictures are concerned? Perhaps he did not use enough technique to say what he had in mind to say. Perhaps, despite this inadequacy, he continues to see in his picture what he intended to put there and does not realize that he failed to do so.

We all have our blind spots, and photographers are no exception, but the ostrich trick is hardly a suitable role for today's photographer. Why not try to face the facts, then do something about them? Make better pictures, pictures that really say what you mean. Admit your failures, discard them—then to work again.

Photographers often allow their feelings about a subject to cloud the issue of technique. Pictures that are essentially fine suffer as a result. They are far less effective and penetrating than they could have been had the photographer tried to make the best use of his materials.

Instead of saying what he means, therefore, his message is greatly weakened—by such factors as the inclusion of irrelevant elements in the picture, the lack of attention to rendering texture and surface values, the failure to integrate the picture elements into one strong, total impression.

Technical errors are frequently due to carelessness, a disregard for basic photographic practice, or a misconception of the factors that contribute to really good photography. I might add, in passing, that incomplete or vague thinking may also result in errors. In such cases, don't forget the demoralization that sets in when you know you are not being effective but you keep going just the same.

However, many of our best photographers feel that an "error" often puts across a visual idea more strongly than strict adherence to basic procedures. On one occasion when this problem was being discussed during a symposium, Lisette Model, one of the finest contemporary photographers in the realistic manner, offered the suggestion that creative photographers may now be on the threshold of a new kind of photography. Perhaps, she added, photographers are finding that they can make pictures more convincing when they feel free of the restrictions imposed by the traditional rules.

Many experiments have been tried in this direction, such as pictures which are unsharp on purpose rather than by accident, deliberate failures of the photographer to stop movement in the subject, and other radical infractions of the rules.

A good many results belong to the "that's-the-way-I-wanted-it" category, but I have seen some that are really very convincing.

Such experiments are an extension of the opinion, and it is one widely held among photographers, that an impression of movement is best achieved if some part of the subject is unsharp due to rapid motion. Even over-all blur (slow shutter) has become acceptable when the effect is sufficiently convincing to justify its use.

Learn to recognize what is relevant in a subject and what is not; what belongs to, and what detracts from, the main theme. First you must understand clearly what you mean to say, then decide on the techniques you will use to say it. Discard everything that weakens the expression and make the principal idea strong by emphasizing its significant features. In the final result, every part of the picture should have a meaning related to the whole.

How Williams Said It

H. I. Williams, top-flight color photographer, was asked to compose a still life to symbolize the place of rubber in the world. How he said what he meant may offer an instructive lesson in thinking out a picture. He was doing a color photograph, but this fact is incidental to our purpose here. The materials he used were colored rubber figures and objects of various shapes. (I use this example because the leisurely nature of the subject allows a detailed and deliberate analysis of how a photographer develops an idea. However, the atmosphere, progression, and logic of the thinking should be generally helpful, whether condensed for a split-second action shot or expanded for a more elaborate subject extending over a considerable period of time.)

Williams started by spreading out his pieces, studying their varied shapes, sizes, and colors, and speculating on the possibilities of each. He invariably rejected all strong colors, because he felt that values were more effective. Gradually, a plan took shape. He would arrange a still life, in which size, form, and space relationship, the juxtaposition of color values, and the use of cast shadows would add up to an idea of a world of rubber. It would have to suggest boundless space, endless time, create a sense of generalization, add here and there a touch of mystery to lure the imagination.

He pushed the items about, moved them in and out of the setting, in and out—for hours—making sure the object shapes did not compete with each other. The criterion of acceptance was: Does the object contribute anything to the result? If the answer was in the negative, out it went. Finally, Williams reached a point where he could neither add nor subtract without hurting the picture. Every object had become an indispensable part of the whole.

Williams planned the placement of colors so that they afforded the necessary contrasts in values. Thus, a white rubber boot provided a logical rallying point for a reddish glove, a multicolored ball, and a pink balloon. A blue water bag added a touch of contrast to the shaded yellow of a rubber animal. Everywhere, he used subtle contrasts in values to promote the feeling of infinity, of "going on forever" that he wanted.

He arranged the objects in perspective, relying partly on distortion and strong foreground shadows to create the illusion of limitless depth. Strong side lighting provided expressive shadows, chiefly to give depth through heavy contrasts, as well as to throw the picture together, connect one object with another, point up significant detail.

You say what you mean when you use techniques in a personal way, like words. Only *you*, the photographer, can breathe life and meaning into them, make them function, give them purpose. That is no light responsibility. It is up to you to use techniques vitally or to misuse them.

You misuse them when you imitate somebody else's work. You misuse them when you follow patterns set up by others. You misuse them when you have nothing to say or when you wilfully distort them or when you fail to make them say what you mean or when you let them say what somebody else says they should mean.

Above all, you are in default when you let the clichés take over instead of using techniques creatively to serve your personal needs.

A "cliché," says Webster, is "a hackneyed expression." That is, it has been done over and over again, and so often that it is no longer an expression in the personal sense but actually a lack, or denial, of expression.

Salon Clichés

To name a few:

The cliché that dictates that you cannot have an empty, or "bald," sky—put clouds in it (even if you have to print them from another negative or rub them in with chalk or crayon). But isn't this a rather sweeping *"don't"* when we know that cloudless skies have meanings too, like the feeling of great calm, the suggestions of loneliness or of vast space? Even the "bald" sky, by which is usually meant a paper-white sky due to extreme overexposure in the camera, has its uses. I once saw a movie in which such a bald sky was used to portray a feeling of stark tragedy.

The cliché that dictates that you must avoid telegraph wires or if you cannot avoid them, remove them during processing. Are you going to stand for that? Telegraph wires are part of our world. Use them. Fit them into the scenes in which they appear. Make them help out your story. Remember, the camera is not a sketching pencil that puts in or leaves out details at will. The camera is a mirror. If you don't like telegraph wires, point your camera elsewhere.

The cliché that dictates (by inference) that still lifes must be the painfully studied arrangements that they are—the deadly perfect groupings of crockery (how do they differ from ordinary commercial shots, except for pictorial technique?) and the piling of fruit in bowls (with a grape or two "dropped" in just the right spot to "lead the eye into the picture"). Why shouldn't a still life really have some life in it, some feeling of movement and suggestion of human interest? Why does it have to be a *display?* Why not a *portrayal* of some real aspect of everyday living?

The cliché that dictates that abstract ideas are most "artistically" symbolized by nude studies. Symbols are all around you, in the subjects that make up our lives, the homely details of the daily round. These you know, and they have meaning, close personal associations. Nudes as they are represented in the salons are in the main symbols of nothing except hazy thinking and perversions of the idea of creativity. Nudes can be, and occasionally are, photographed with imagination and creative insight, but such examples are rare.

The cliché that dictates that "genre" pictures must be so self-consciously "arty" that the subject looks like a museum piece rather than the live person he or she is, doing an ordinary job of work. You know the subject has been posed because the result doesn't *look* genuine. Pictures of people doing things—genre, if you wish—should be taken candid-style in a snapshot while the person is actually working, and if it can possibly be arranged, without his being aware of the camera.

The cliché that dictates the boy-with-straw-hat-and-fishing-pole kind of picture as an idea of boy life—especially when set up indoors! It's not the subject so much as the oversentimentalized way in which it is usually handled . . . Let us photograph boys as boys, doing things boys do normally, and let them act naturally. Boys are real persons; don't photograph them as bric-a-brac.

The cliché that dictates the "winding-road" notion of landscapes, snow scenes, etc. The deadly monotony of such subject matter and the manner in which it is treated has probably done more to retard picture making along creative lines than any other single influence. The pastoral theme has been so overworked that it has achieved the unfavorable appellation of "calendar art." Yet the subject has real possibilities when approached with understanding.

The drawback to real thinking here is that photographers are too prone to view a scene merely as a winding road and by this token to photograph it chiefly because it falls into a category, the category of the S curve that is the delight of every pictorialist's eye. But life is more than just an S curve. Shoot your S curve—it is essentially a beautiful line—but put something in it. Give it a meaning relating to your ideas about living things. The winding road, the running brook, the tree by the wayside—they are all *essentially* significant in the over-all scheme of life, provoking responses from us that vary with environment, temperament, and our thinking at any given time and place. Forget categoric clichés. Look inside yourself and photograph what you want to say—*your* way.

The cliché that dictates the unrealistic approach to child photography by which children are caricatured rather than portrayed. Children dressed in cute costumes to represent other children rather than themselves, to cite one frequent example. Children made to assume attributes of adults, such as the desire to kiss each other (one such picture, of a little boy and girl kissing, won a $1,000 prize in a national contest, thus giving sanction to further picture making in this vein). Children don't *do* such things. Why do adults insist on photographing them in such unreal situations, when there are so many wonderful aspects of child life that haven't even been touched? Study children; get to know them better. They're nice people. They live in a little world of their own, with problems of their own, needs, interests, ideas of their own. Look in on this world.

Photograph it understandingly. But don't impose your adult ideas on its inhabitants. When you do that, your photographs of them are untrue. They are photographs that reflect *your* world rather than *theirs*.

The cliché that dictates "character studies" rather than studies of character. Avoid the basic error of differentiating between people and "characters." You know—you've seen them on exhibition walls time and again—"The Old Vendor," "Sea Captain," "Apache," etc. All these are people too, not mere "characters." The fact that the Vendor has a beard and the Captain a goatee, that the Captain has a weather-beaten face and the Apache is smooth and dark, does not exclude them from the category of people. Photograph them as people, not as waxen images of something you dreamed up for the sole purpose of exhibiting your artistry. Every portrait you take should be your interpretation of that person's character, not merely a "pleasing expression," cajoled out of the subject for the sake of the picture, or a simulated idea of the person. Get to know the subject as an individual; learn the particular attributes that distinguish his personality from other personalities. Dig out the special features about him that yield themselves to photography, like mannerisms, gestures, facial expressions. Art photographers try to give the impression that they are photographing the "soul" of the subject. Can't be done. You photograph only the visual signs that indicate to you the kind of person he is. And this goes for every kind of person without exception, including so-called "characters."

But suppose you take it from here. You probably know a few clichés yourself.

Clichés flourish in an atmosphere of mental and emotional stagnation. They exist only by grace of inaction. Photographers allow themselves to be ruled by clichés when they forfeit opportunities to photograph creatively, when they choose the easy road of conformity rather than the harder one that calls for initiative and a search for real values reflecting their person-alities.

Clichés are a state of mind—a static state. You can change clichés to original thinking simply by changing your view-point, by thinking on your feet and making pictures to suit yourself instead of following a formula. Once you have changed to the new viewpoint and have experienced the deep satisfaction inherent in the new freedom, the clichés won't stand a chance. You will be on your own—and like it.

Only then will you really be able to say what you mean, and say it with the confidence of a personal conviction arrived at by examining your own reactions to subject matter.

It seems obvious that you cannot say what you mean when you submit to clichés that tell you what to say. The clichés tell you to do this but not to do the other. They make it easy, because you don't have to solve any problems yourself. Every picture problem is solved for you in advance; just follow the rules.

That would be feasible if life itself were a fixed formula. But how can you work by rules when life is always on the move and your relationship to life is constantly changing? How can you answer problems at one period in your life in the same way that you do at other times and under other circum-stances?

You can take the same pictures at fifty that you take at twenty by following a handy list of clichés, but you will not be saying what you mean. How can you? Surely, thirty years must make *some* difference in your thinking. You will mean something else at fifty, if you have grown at all. And if you don't say it the new way, then the clichés have got you—but good.

What have those clichés to do with life, anyway?

I ask *you*.

CHAPTER EIGHT

Use Techniques as Words

The more important the story, the better the photographer should try to tell it. The more powerful the picture, the more certain I am that people will have a chance to understand what I want to say.

W. EUGENE SMITH

WHAT ROLE HAVE you assigned to technique in your photography? Is technique your master or your servant? Are you using technique or being used by it?

It makes a difference.

Technique is your servant—as it should be always—when you use it to realize or to strengthen a picture idea rather than for its own sake. Technique becomes your master when you employ it as the end result rather than as the vehicle for your expression.

Take the case of Alfred Stieglitz, for example. His studies of hands render skin values so truthfully that the hands seem to come alive. This despite obvious technical flaws, such as subject movement. For Stieglitz used technique when he needed it, ignored it when it served his purpose to do so. The pictures

87

in some of our best salons are sharp; tone values are nicely modulated in strict accordance with the book of rules; technique is achieved without a fault. But the feeling and warmth of living things that Stieglitz captured have been lost in the process.

The general impression today's photographer can gain from a study of Stieglitz's pictures is that they combine technique and subject matter in such a way that technique is subordinated to the theme. The fault in much of today's photography is that emphasis is shifted to technique, and the excellence with which a print is turned out assumes greater importance than the subject matter itself instead of the other way about.

How does one measure a photographer's ability? Certainly not merely by the yardstick of technical competence. The difference between one photographer and another is not that simple. We should inquire into the ability of each to *interpret* as well as to *apply* the techniques he knows. We should be curious about the way in which a photographer reconciles the principles of good craftsmanship with meaningful photographic expression. We should expect of the "better" photographer superiority of judgment as to what is important and what is trivial, keener responsiveness, a more confident use of techniques. When the subject calls for it, he should have the intelligence and the courage to alter or even to go counter to the established rules in order to make a photographic statement of maximum significance.

Above all, our better photographer will have nothing to do with the cliché catechism by which less adventurous and less imaginative photographers allow themselves to be ruled. (In the preceding chapter I called attention to some of the more glaring of the clichés governing subject matter and its treatment. I refer to others elsewhere in this book, and in succeeding chapters I discuss clichés relating to some of the basic problems applicable in all photography. In the present chapter, I hope to cover aspects relating to print making, print finishing, and print mounting and to try to show how the clichés may be combated by any photographer who is willing to try. It is here that photographers reveal their full intention and achieve, or fail to achieve, the unity of expression discussed in Chapter 6, "Have Something to Say.")

Paper Surface

To record the finest detail, nothing is better than a glossy-paper surface. This is fact. Yet its use is frowned upon by exhibition judges, even in the case of pictures that actually demand a glossy paper to tell their story most effectively. This is one of the most unfair and senseless of the print clichés because hardly any attempt is made to justify it by giving consideration to the suitability of the surface to the subject portrayed. Prints are voted out *merely* because they are printed on glossy paper.

One reason I assume for the taboo on glossy paper is that the surface is unsuitable for some of the pictorial "control" processes. But this objection does not hold water—because the kind of subject matter which prints best on glossy paper does not lend itself to anything but straight printing.

On the other hand, rough-surface and other textured papers are quite respectable. This, despite the fact that the texture of the paper calls attention to itself, blunts the outlines of the photographic image and smudges the delicate gradations of tone! What does it avail to nurse a negative carefully through the developing process, when you do all this to it afterward?

In the same spirit is the use of a screen to add a fine over-all pattern to the print. The most amazing example of the kind I know was described with pride by the photographer who "saved" a picture of a nude figure with skin discolorations by printing the image through a lace pattern!

A semimatte- or a matte-surface paper will allow the photographer to print any subject he wants to (short of those which print better on glossy paper) if he has a good negative to start with. But to use a coarse-textured paper in order to hide image defects or to get an "artistic" result is not the kind of photographic practice that helps expression. Rather, it tends to distort.

Print Size

The story of conformity is told eloquently on exhibition walls and in club contests. Nothing less than a 14 by 17 or 16 by 20-inch print will do. Makes a better impression on the judges, you know. How could you expect to win with anything less?

It is encouraging to see, however, that quite a number of photographers are turning to 11 by 14 inches and occasionally even to 8 by 10. "To me photography is a very intimate thing," one photographer has said. "Anything larger than 11 by 14 inches disturbs this quality and hurts the picture."

But it is not just a matter of size for the sake of size only. But what size print for what *particular subject?* A 14 by 17-inch size hurts *what* picture?

It is not generally appreciated that print size is an aspect of expression. You say things with print size too, and with format. Something like big rooms and small rooms. Objects appropriate for the first may be entirely unsuitable for the second. Furniture intended for a small room may not only be smaller but also daintier in character than furniture intended for a big room.

It is the same way with small prints and large ones. There should be no such thing as a standard size. The print size should be considered in its relation to the subject matter and the mood and message it is intended to convey. If the print is too big, it may kill the intimate treatment demanded by the subject matter. But where the photographer wants to depict the idea of space, a larger print might be more fitting. A small print would compress the area so that the notion of open space would not be apparent.

Print Format

The subject matter dictates the format. Don't standardize your print sizes merely because the paper is cut to standard sizes by the manufacturer. It's the picture that counts. Give the picture a chance to specify its own format. The shape of the format you employ may help your story or weaken it. After all, format is one more medium at your command to make your statement as clear as possible. The wrong format may even cause some confusion in the observer as to exactly what it is you are trying to get across.

Arnold Newman makes the rather extreme suggestion that photographers try experimenting with cutouts of images pasted on mounting board. I don't think we need go that far to make formats contribute their share in the shaping of a picture. But have you ever tried printing a tall subject, like high city buildings or a high summit or a waterfall, within a tall, narrow format? Or printing with a shallow horizontal format a landscape or seascape or some other subject in which significant content stretched horizontally over a very wide area? Such narrow formats can be made to accent the ideas of space constriction, length, and height and thus intensify the meaning of the subject.

Print Toning

The cliché of arbitrarily changing the color of a print, by toning it chemically in a separate bath after development or doing so directly with a paper-and-developer combination during development, is a fixture in the salons, though now, happily, used less than formerly. Employed in this promiscuous way, toning is meaningless, but toning can add feeling to a picture if used for a purpose. A group of small portraits I recall was greatly improved by treatment in a gold-toning solution. They became warmer and had an antique feeling that suited the background and the subject depicted—a bewhiskered old man.

Toning need not be carried all the way. Many photographers use toning only to brighten the over-all contrast of the print, not to give the print a new color. Whether you tone a print or leave it alone, retaining photographic quality should be your chief technical objective. Too frequently, the toned print loses something in the process, due to the fact that the new brown or blue color not only adds little to the meaning of the picture but in certain cases actually is inconsistent with the nature of the subject.

Print toning is an automatic step in the processing routine of a good many amateur photographers, largely because it is expected of them. This is just one of the cases where technique has gotten the better of the photographer: he does not think in terms of directing the toning technique to serve his creative ends but uses it as a matter of course because that's the way it's

This picture for *Life* by David Douglas Duncan of Turkish cavalry on maneuvers is undoubtedly one of the greatest in contemporary photography. Caught at just the right moment, an instant of unique vision, it has epic quality.

The charm of this evocative impression of an empty circus tent by
Sol Libsohn is principally one of mood and suggestion. It is a picture
for continued and thoughtful looking, emotionally, nostalgically.

94

This picture by Alfred Eisenstaedt is not merely a strong composition, drawing the eye as with a powerful magnet up the balustrade. Eisenstaedt is sharing his amazement at the beauty of the design.

Here is a striking example of a commercial shot that achieves an imaginative "portrait" of a chair. Tom Leonard used his masterful technique and economy of means to endow a chair with personality.

A deeply religious quality pervades this moving domestic scene by Harold Feinstein. The principal interest is, of course, in the sunlit curtains, with their strong Biblical feeling and naive, primitive design.

The popular conception of retirement is summed up in this highly articulate impression by Morris Gordon. It is a somewhat depressing picture, but for too many retired persons unfortunately a true one.

$\longrightarrow$

Lawrence Shustak closed in on this detail at a folk singers' festival both because of its simple design and its symbolic expression. Here form and line are used effectively for unusual composition.

done. Many take it for granted that an exhibition print should be toned. A frequent question is, "What tones shall I use?" instead of, "I wonder if toning will help me make this picture better understood?"

Toning often is employed to hide technical faults, such as extreme flatness of contrast, and for no other reason. The trick is seldom successful. The mere presence of the color does not help or detract; it only adds to the poor quality of the original work, sometimes making the picture even worse than it would have been if left untoned. Don't use toning to "save" a print. That is not the function of toning. Start from scratch instead; make a new print.

A prevalent toning cliché in the salons is that snow scenes and night scenes should be toned blue. The explanation usually given is that in the case of the first, the shadows are blue, and in the case of both, the blue tone helps to promote a characteristic cold feeling. Similarly, water is toned blue, sometimes green.

What's wrong with the basic values of black and white? Isn't the scale of gray values a more truthful means of rendering these subjects? After all, snow is white, not blue. And even if one were to grant the justice of using a blue tone because the shadows are blue (which, incidentally, is not apparent to the human eye to anything like the extent shown in blue-toned prints), how about the surrounding objects, like trees, houses, or bridges? They are dark grays, browns, or even blacks. Then why change them to blue?

Because that is the way the judges want it, of course. To the juror steeped in the prejudices of tradition, an untoned snow scene is an incomplete print. Some judges feel the same way about night scenes that are not toned blue, though the night is dominantly black.

Toning as a technique can be valuable in helping to fill

out and point up meaning in a picture. But it is misused when other motives, such as salon acceptance, guide the photographer's thinking.

Print "Color"

By this term we usually mean the "warmth" or "coldness" of a print. A "warm" print has softly graded, diffused tone values, with the over-all print color tending toward warm black (soft, slightly brown) or brown, due to the paper and developer used, not to actual toning. A "cold" print is black or blue-black, offering brighter contrasts. All these values must be given consideration by the photographer who is anxious to say what he means in the most effective ways at his command. To be fully articulate photographically, he must know when to use a warm-tone paper and soft development and when to use the colder tone of black in order, for example, to emphasize the idea of bright contrast in a subject.

In order to have complete personal control of the results, photographers should, in most cases, start with a white-paper stock and build up values in accordance with their interpretation of a subject. White, rather than buff or ivory, paper is particularly necessary when the photographer intends to use toning to complete his picture.

Print Mounting

The pictorialist has practically no problems on the score of mounting. The clichés dictate a 16 by 20-inch mount, hung vertically. So all you have to do is mount the print on standard-size mounting cardboard and leave the rest to fate. If you have made your print in the same spirit of conformity, fate will be kind. Your print will hang. At least, your chances will be very good.

Why must all mounts be 16 by 20, and why must they all hang vertically? Maybe an interior decorator could answer that question better than I can, because it certainly has little to do with the good photographer's thesis—personal expressiveness. But I'll try.

The utilitarian reason is fairly obvious: it is more convenient to hang mounts of the same size and shape than it is to arrange mounts of different sizes. But utility is not the sole motive here. To me, the 16 by 20-inch mount is the crowning triumph of the forces of conformity. It is the symbol of the imposed sameness of thought that dogs the photographer at every step and discourages his individuality.

The practice among contemporary photographers interested in making their pictures along original lines is to let the picture itself suggest the mount. The motivation is the same as in the case of the print format, that is, to make the mount round out the story the photographer is trying to tell. There is a marked tendency to have the mount the same size as the print, without white borders. Another method is to mount small prints on large mounts. Mount sizes therefore vary widely.

This variety makes the task of displaying prints more than just a straight hanging job. Each print must be given the maximum opportunity to deliver its message. It should be related in some way—subject, mood, treatment—to other pictures on the wall. Thus, the effort to tell a clear and convincing story may be carried through even the final stage of print hanging. This last phase of picture presentation has received too little attention in the handling of exhibitions.

Print Quality

When photographers have something to say and have enough techniques to say it with, then print quality becomes a means of communication rather than an empty exercise, or worse, a fetish substitute for imagination.

"Print quality" is the term usually applied to describe the over-all technical perfection of a photograph—or the lack of it. Thus, we approve or disapprove of a print by saying that the print has "good" or "bad" print quality. Where we miss out, though, is that we are too prone to stop there, without trying to see how well or ill the photographer has employed the technique to give meaning to the subject matter.

The print may have good quality but little to justify its use. Or it may be poor in quality yet have feeling, or meaning, that gets across to the observer despite its faults. I have noticed, however, that most pictures that have something worthwhile to say also have good, or at least acceptable, print quality and that bad-quality prints also show bad-quality thinking.

Proficiency in making prints comes gradually as the result of the photographer's growing desire to say things well in pictures. A strong need to communicate his ideas and impressions persuasively inspires the photographer to learn, and then he relates technique to meaning so that the two fuse into the single effort called "expression."

The more the photographer develops his abilities along creative lines, the less he is concerned with consciously trying to distinguish between technique and meaning. Constant improvement in print quality becomes equivalent to clarifying his thinking. His print quality becomes better not merely because he knows more technique but because he knows more about life and more about himself and is therefore able to say more accurately what he thinks.

When you learn to appreciate print quality in this way, you make pictures that are sharp or diffused, contrasty or with the tone values well graduated, not because you like to make such pictures but because you choose the effect best suited to tell a particular story in a particular way. How can we say that *every* picture must have detail in the shadows and detail in the highlights, any more than we can say that every picture must be soft focus or every picture must be very sharp? Such blanket statements are unrealistic because they do not relate to creativity.

You may work in only one of these methods and succeed very well in expressing your thoughts on photographic paper, but that may be because you prefer working within the limitations of a specific approach. Thus, you may want all your pictures sharp because you feel you are more articulate when you point up the significance of detail. On the other hand, you may wish to make your picture soft because you feel atmosphere is the most important factor in a picture. There are many instances of photographers who find they can work with both these approaches or more, adapting their technique to the situation in hand.

The important thing for a photographer to remember is that he needs to express his idea in the best way. He should not try to work to a fixed formula but should change his means as often as necessary to fit his ends. People who say that no picture is good if it is not first of all a sharp picture do not understand the true meaning of print quality, which is to use technique like words. A carefully enunciated word may not be nearly so effective as a colloquial usage of the word. The one may leave the listener cold and untouched; the other, stir him to response.

It is the same with techniques. A sharp, full-scaled print may be the rule, but if an unsharp print tells a stronger story, give me that one. At the same time, however, I expect the photographer who makes the unsharp picture to convince me that what he has to say could not have been said better by any other means.

Print quality, then, is perfection of the *means of expression* rather than merely of technique. A picture has good print quality when it shows evidence that those means have been used with intelligent purpose. Print quality is the flowering of a photographic idea conceived and executed with imagination and insight.

CHAPTER NINE

What Holds It Together?

> *I get a greater joy from finding things in nature,
> already composed, than I do from my finest per-
> sonal arrangements. . . . Then so-called "com-
> position" becomes a personal thing to be devel-
> oped along with technique as a personal way of
> seeing.*
>
> EDWARD WESTON

IN A WORD: *idea.*

Idea—that is what holds a picture together.

An idea pulls together all the pieces in the picture and holds them as if they were but one.

Not "composition," according to the book of rules.

"Composition is only the strongest way of seeing," Edward Weston replied, when asked to define the term.

Definitions of this kind never satisfy photographers who work by formulas. They want specific directions they can follow. Weston's definition leaves the question up to the pho-tographer—to answer for himself every time he comes face to face with his subject and must decide what *is* "the strongest way of seeing" that particular subject.

Formula photographers prefer a set of rules—the spatial rule of thirds, the rule of the leading line, etc. For them composition is a kind of mold, an inflexible form into which you pour the image. When it "sets," the image becomes a picture, or so they firmly believe.

Composition is not a static mold but a flowing, living element in the photograph by which each part is made to contribute to other parts and all are bound together by a single dominating theme. When all the parts have become integrated, the picture is complete, the photographer has made a full statement, and the observer understands what the photographer has tried to say.

A complete picture is one in which all the space is well accounted for—no area without significance, no part to make the observer wonder why a detail was not included. Everything has purpose and meaning.

The photographer who works by the conventional rules of composition and never dares to change one of them, even though he feels the infraction might help the picture along, is fighting shy of creativity. His "composition" may be letter perfect, but his message will prove obscure and uninspiring because he leaves out something he wants to say or says something in a way he does not mean to say it.

For example, the rules say that the horizon line in a landscape or a seascape should never be placed in the center of the picture. It should be either a third of the way up from the bottom or a third of the way down from the top (the "rule of thirds"). The only liberty permitted is a slight shift, up or down, in the position of the line.

But suppose a photographer sees something in the scene that just will not fit this formula? Suppose he feels he could make a more personal statement by pushing the horizon clear to the top or to the bottom edge of the picture? Then what? Well, he has the choice of forcing his idea to fit the rule, thus abandoning his inspiration, or he can follow his own thinking even though he knows he will have to defend his "crime" at the next camera-club show.

Here is a story that typifies the viewpoint of the conformist in this connection:

A prominent magazine photographer was being "pumped" on her methods by a group of amateurs, whose luncheon guest she was. Somebody brought up the subject of composition. He wanted to know how she composed her pictures.

"That depends on a lot of things," she replied, "on the subject, the idea I want to put across in the picture. I just take the most interesting angle to get the most effective picture, that's all."

But this was not what the young man wanted; he yearned for "how-to" information. He placed a piece of paper on the table and offered her a pencil. "Now let's say this is the film. Where would you put the tree?"

She was bewildered and amused. "What tree and where? How do I know where I would put *a* tree? I would put it where it belonged, where it would help my story. But how can I tell you without seeing the subject?"

It was very plain to her questioner, though. He would put it one-third from the left side of the picture or one-third from the right. *He* did not have to see the subject to know that much. For wasn't that one of the time-honored rules? All you have to do is just follow the rules, and you can't go wrong—*he* thought. It never occurred to him that the rules might be questioned and even broken if the subject called for some other treatment.

Rules Questioned

The rules *have* been questioned—by a machine. Lloyd E. Varden, widely known photographic technician and authority and an uncompromising critic of pictorialist tradition, has made known the following results of scientific investigation:

"Leading" lines do not lead, and "distracting" areas do not divert your attention when you view photographs, according to his reports. Evidence provided by a motion-picture "eye camera," which records the movements of the human eye as it examines a picture, shows that the usual rules of composition have little basis in fact. Yet prints continue to be made and their value appraised according to the rules.

The eye camera is a 16mm motion-picture camera which photographs the movements of the eye as illuminated by a small beam of light. It records the eye positions, or "fixation points," several times each second. When these exposures are charted and the fixation points established, the result is an accurate record of the places where the eye rested during a 20- to 30-second examination of the picture. The camera is employed chiefly in psychological studies, where its use was introduced by Mr. Varden.

Photographers speak of the need for establishing "lines of movement" in pictures, through such devices as a curve in a road or a rope line, to lead the eye of the observer along a fixed path to the area or areas of chief interest. However, by actual test with the eye camera, in which several persons viewed the same picture successively, the eye was shown to ignore these lines and to follow an erratic course.

It was observed that the eye went immediately to the position thought to be the center of interest, without following any "leading" lines. This despite the fact, Mr. Varden says, that the observers were all pictorialists of high standing, who make and judge photographs on the basis of the accepted rules.

Photographers also are taught that extraneous material in a composition, particularly in strong-light areas, tends to draw attention away from the main subject. It is said to detract from the total effect produced by any picture. As a result, photographers are careful to avoid strong highlights in unimportant areas so as to keep the interest centered on a particular section. Many resort to darkening corners of the print.

These and other "disturbing" details, to which reference is frequently made in photographic criticism, seem not to exist, however, when examined by the eye camera. The tests showed that many such details did not for a moment catch the interest of the observer, even when the observer was a judge who ordinarily would condemn a photograph because of them.

Whenever there was a strong center of interest, the eye did not roam appreciably except after long periods of observation. In one picture, a highlighted area in one corner did not cause the eye to be distracted from the chief point of interest at any time during the course of inspection.

So now we have even the word of science to tell us that things are not always as they seem to the book of rules. Of course, we must consider the viewpoint—the characteristic objectivity of the scientific approach, which operates on the basis of measurable facts only and disregards the factor of a personal impression. That the eye goes directly to the center of interest sounds logical without having to be proved, but still it can appreciate the presence of attractive "leading" lines, even though not led by them.

It is comforting to have science on the side of progress in

photography. However, I think more important than the "debunking" of the rules is the point Mr. Varden tried to make, namely, that photographers should recognize that blind devotion to the rules discourages fresh viewpoints.

I believe that the principal fault lies in the fact that too many photographers start with the rules rather than with an idea, a worthwhile incentive to take a picture. Photographers are inclined to look for compositions rather than story material. They see "arrangements," "leading lines," or some other cliché and shoot pictures for the sake of the composition rather than for any other values they may have.

A photographer can improve his pictures merely by reversing this procedure. If he will look for pictures instead of compositions, then try to understand the subject and shoot accordingly, it will be just a matter of making his meaning clear; the "pleasing" arrangement will take care of itself in the process.

Philippe Halsman, the magazine illustrator, believes in making composition an instinctive part of his technique. He does a good deal of experimenting with a variety of subjects, in order to teach his eyes to sense composition quickly and to respond with a fine sense of timing. He starts with a well-defined conception of what he is after, then arranges and lights the material accordingly, and shoots at the right moment. First the idea; *then* the composition.

Space Ideas

Amateurs should concern themselves much more than they now do with ideas of space. The interpretation of space is a fascinating subject and a challenge both to the imagination and the photographer's technical abilities. Photographers have done some work in this field, but seldom is it approached with enough breadth of vision to do it full justice.

Most pictures in which space interpretation is attempted fall far short of their goal because the photographer crowds the subject too much, does not allow it enough room to "breathe." Also, the problem of perspective is not considered adequately. As a result, many such pictures turn out to be "general views" rather than visualizations of space. The photographer fails to get into the picture any impression of spatial depth.

Here the photographer who has the courage to set himself free of established taboos can gain a rich harvest of personal satisfaction and achievement. He should try to capture such ideas as the feeling of the littleness of things and persons in the great outdoors, the atmosphere of infinite distance, or the mystery suggested by a deep recession of alternate lights and darks in a huge interior. These subjects must be felt strongly and thought out carefully to achieve the desired results.

Amateurs think of space as areas in a picture that must be filled—with a figure, object, etc. Empty space can be useful too, and by the power of suggestion, far more dramatic. A very small figure in space can point up the emptiness and vastness of open landscape through contrast. However, do not merely put in a figure; have it relate to the space in some way, give it some reason for being there. Many pictures are puzzling because a figure is included arbitrarily for the single purpose of breaking up a large expanse of space rather than because the photographer has tried to say something about what that figure is doing there, what its relationship is to the whole.

There is "small" space as well as "great" space, and the opportunities for using it are also interesting and challenging. Let air into your picture, get separation between the planes, work for depth, emphasize the atmosphere of a third dimension. Don't hesitate to allow space around a portrait, for example. It isn't necessary always to fill every bit of area with *things*. Leave some space for the imagination of the observer to move around in, the better to understand the subject portrayed. Photographers have achieved highly expressive effects by a generous and intelligent use of space values.

How Much Is Enough?

Another common fault with amateurs is their tendency to include too much in the picture and their failure to realize that a picture with too much in it is a vague picture. Because the photographer makes no attempt to select only one of the several aspects of the subject, his print carries little meaning or importance.

A close-up of a detail frequently reveals more of the subject than a picture of the whole subject. Photographers too often take general views because the subject offers "good composition," an attractive lighting effect, or a record of some kind. The near view can be more interesting and useful because of the interpretive values the photographer is obliged to introduce. The isolated part can tell more, be more emphatic, more quickly appreciated and understood. It tells the story in compressed, sometimes dramatic, terms, using economy of expression to point up a specific idea with greatest effect.

For example, the doorway of an old house, properly lighted and photographed from the most interesting point of view, may give a better idea of the house's age and associations than a picture of the entire building. One individual in a group, picked out for a close-up because he is typical of the rest, may give a clearer understanding of what the group is like than a picture of the full group.

And so with details of a ship, a section of a building, a part of a bridge, a single flower, or any comparatively small, isolated subject. Through his efforts to select particular segments of subject matter and to photograph them one by one rather than together, the photographer makes clear for others the meaning of the subject as he understands it.

"Composition as such should not be a conscious consideration in the making of pictures," says Edward B. Kaminski, Los Angeles teacher. "In approaching the subject, decide how much of it you want to include in the picture. If there is anything in the picture area that detracts from the theme, move in closer to eliminate it; if not enough, move back to include more." When the photographer knows what he wants, the needed details fall naturally into place, and "composition" is achieved.

He offers a practical suggestion: "I have found this procedure most effective with my students: First, shoot a large scene, then close in on it and cut it in half. Close in again and again until, finally, you isolate the most important subject and thus make a statement about the main thing in the scene. In this way, you learn, bit by bit, that lots of things you see in a picture are really unimportant, and so you learn how to select the part or parts that are most meaningful."

Integrating the Picture

Integration of the several elements in a picture and of the associated factors of print quality, format, etc. (discussed in Chapter 8, "Use Techniques as Words") is the goal of the photographer who wishes to make a unified photographic statement. It clarifies for him and emphasizes for others the aspects in his picture that have the greatest significance.

"Integration" refers to the evaluation by the photographer of each phase of picture making on the basis of maximum visual understanding. In this process of evaluation, he should guard against making decisions by rules and practices only. As in the selection of subject matter, viewpoint, and other picture-taking factors, so in print making, the photographer should learn to rely on his own judgment, because nobody knows better than he does what he is trying to say.

Thus, a photographer will automatically darken the corners of his print in order to keep the subject from "running out of the picture." Why not, instead, work to present the subject itself so effectively that the eye of the observer is not tempted to leave it? Then darken the corners, if you find you need to, for some other reason, like mood or import. Darkening corners for the purpose of enclosing the center of interest sometimes is equivalent to trying to force the observer to look at the picture whether he wants to or not. In many instances, too, the darkened corners actually are a detriment; they hedge the subject in, tend to stifle the intended fuller expression.

Another aspect that must be taken into account in integration is the differentiation between "distracting" elements in a picture and those which contribute to it. Disregarding the "opinion" of the machine we quoted a while back, a picture should be complete in every respect. A harsh light spot in one corner, which adds nothing to the meaning, should not be there. Because it is extraneous, it may actually detract from the meaning. Unrelated lines, waste-space areas, pointless details, all tend to weaken the total impression.

In the same way, study other elements in the picture, but always from the viewpoint of meaning rather than rules, of how they fit into the picture in question rather than how they fit into a pattern. Photographers who have studied the rules of composition often have the smug feeling that they know all about it: "You just follow the rules." The better photographers know that composition is more than that—it is a matter of feeling rather than of rules learned by rote; that you develop this feeling as you go along; and that you never really "know it all" because, as you learn more about life, you put emphasis on different things. For composition is just another way of looking at life.

CHAPTER TEN

Consider Light

By lighting alone, a photographer can impart his special poetry of mood, intensifying or suppressing as does the stage designer.

BARBARA MORGAN

THE AMATEUR SEEMS to develop a kind of psychological block whenever he attempts indoor pictures by artificial light. This, despite the simplicity of the medium and the wide distribution of literature on the subject. Outdoors, however, he feels perfectly at home. No lights to set up. No matter what kind of lighting he has, pictures can be taken. Whereas indoors he must observe certain rules to avoid getting "inky" shadows and harshly lighted faces, outdoors he has better success with less knowledge. He simply points the camera and shoots whenever the light "looks" right on the subject.

Unfortunately, he seems to be less concerned with light, as the factor that has most to do with how his subject will look in the print, than he is with the mechanical factor of exposure. Photographic literature promotes this attitude by making a point of including exposure data in picture captions. This information has little practical value, and could well be dispensed with for the much more constructive statement of the photographer's motive in taking the picture.

Lighting is not used creatively to the extent that it used to be. Despite the great variety of lighting equipment and artificial light sources, quality in illumination is subordinated to purely mechanical skill in the handling of light sources. We delight in equipment but make little effort to use it to make our picture ideas more expressive of our thinking.

Paul L. Anderson, of East Orange, New Jersey, author of a standard work on pictorial techniques, has suggested that photographers combine the beauty of light, as it was appreciated and recorded by the Photo Secessionists (see Chapter 18, "Lessons at Exhibits"), with records of life's incidents.

"The camera possesses two abilities which no other medium of expression can equal," he wrote me. "First, it can reproduce perfectly the gradations of light on surfaces and can thus express the infinite beauty of these gradations, which other mediums merely suggest; second, it can capture and record, as no other medium can, the passing show of life—the incidents which go to make up the world about us.

"The Photo Secessionists exploited the first ability to the limit. Some of the Photo Secessionists combined with their statement of passing events a very fine feeling for the first ability of the camera, to record the beauty of light.

"Now, why should not the present-day workers, with their present technical facilities far in advance of what the Photo Secessionists had, work in the second manner, as they do, but at the same time make use of the first power of the camera? It seems that in their enthusiasm for the second form of expression they have entirely lost sight of the first; certainly many if not most of the salon prints of today are definitely ugly in their indifference to the quality of light, and certainly it would mean much hard study to develop the two impressions in one picture.

"But it has been done. It would be something worthwhile to see some of the more active workers of today combine the two forms."

Anderson was thinking of daylight, but his suggestion should apply to lighting by artificial sources as well. If only we could convince our photographers that it is they, not their lighting equipment, who control the picture, we would have more stress on the creative effort we so badly need today.

It is a temptation for most amateurs to reason that if they equip themselves with the same kind of elaborate lights that the professionals use, they will then, as a matter of course, produce pictures with professional quality lighting. This, of course, is not necessarily true.

Lighting Is Basic

The principles of artificial illumination are basically the same, regardless of the cost or elaborateness of the equipment. An inexpensive pair of reflectors with ordinary flood lamps will do the same job as a much more complicated, more powerful, and more expensive lighting set.

The bigger, more complex lights are essential for the professional photographer because of the demands of the jobs on which the lights are used. He needs great light output, complete flexibility of lighting units. The amateur works on a far smaller scale to pursue essentially similar aims, namely, a faithful rendering of the subject.

When the amateur switches from simple flood lamps to a more elaborate set and a spotlight, he is motivated largely by the greater convenience and extended possibilities the better equipment offers but partly, too, by a desire to imitate the professional's methods. Such a step is logical for the amateur who has outgrown the limitations of the simpler outfit. But if he makes the change before he is ready for it, on the assumption that his pictures will automatically be better lighted, then he may find himself in trouble. Without a reasonable mastery of the fundamentals, more and better lights will only prove a handicap.

A fundamental lighting scheme should aim to reproduce in the print some idea of the solidity and roundness of the subject. This illusion is achieved by an appropriate distribution of light and shadow areas. Whether the subject be a person, an object, or a group, the problem is the same.

To get this roundness and solidity, two lights are used, one at a 45-degree angle and slightly above the subject, to create a highlight on one side of the face and a shadow on the other. The second light is placed near or next to the camera and directed toward the shadow area to provide just enough illumination to balance but not equal the effect of the first, or key, light. The result, as seen from the camera position, should show a well-modeled subject, that is, one with depth and form.

In order to achieve this inequality of light strength between the key light and the front light, the latter must either be weaker or placed farther from the subject than the former. When you double the distance to the light source, the camera exposure must be increased four times, and so forth.

This, in brief, is the basic artificial lighting method which, with some variations, produces well-lighted photographs. It works effectively no matter what the light source used—flood, flash, or speedlight. It also explains, by intimation, why daylight photography is by comparison so easy and foolproof: the source of the lighting—the sun—is so far from the subject that for all practical purposes the light is always at the same "distance."

Three Lighting Methods

Today's methods of lighting by artificial sources may conveniently be divided into three categories: arranged, utility, and casual. The first refers to the planned lighting setup, whether professional or amateur, and includes all types of photographic light sources—flash, flood, or speedlight. The second refers specifically to the use of a flash gun on the camera —either for the sake of convenience and readiness, as in press work, or because the gun is fixed on the camera and cannot be used any other way, as in the increasing number of inexpensive flash cameras. The third refers to the accidental or existing lighting in public places, such as restaurants, sports arenas, at outdoor festivals, near store windows, etc.

The flash gun on the camera, aimed straight at the subject, produces an image every time, but one that is generally lacking in good modeling. (This is not always true, but it is with many amateur efforts.) In any event, no matter how good the result, a better one could have been achieved with the light source a little to one side of the subject. However, in the case of the press photographer, who often works under difficulties and must get his picture quickly or not at all, the flash gun fixed on the camera is, of course, a necessity.

There is no such excuse, however, for photographers working on feature assignments for newspapers and magazines to use this method. The best cameramen in these fields almost always have an extension cord which allows them to take the gun off the camera and hold it up at some approximation of the 45-degree angle. In addition, many photographers frequently use multiple flash sources carefully arranged according to the principles employed by the studios.

The speedlight method, colloquially, though erroneously, called "strobe," has been making rapid headway as an aid in shooting subjects as varied as small children and dancers. Its advantage lies chiefly in the fact that a single tube, or lamp, can be flashed thousands of times and at very high speeds, like $\frac{1}{1000}$ second or faster. To date, the speedlight has served chiefly as an effective means of stopping high-speed action and shooting babies and has proved itself useful in scientific research. On occasion it has served the creative worker.

The Casual Approach

The category of the casual is the happy hunting ground of the candid photographer and the documentarian. These workers find in the normal lightings of public places just the kind of illumination they need for the unposed scenes they like to photograph. Because the lighting is so diffuse, the light reaching any one area is rather weak, requiring a fast lens and fast film at slow shutter speeds.

Snapshots made under such casual lightings have an authentic flavor that is unmatched by arranged illumination. People are more natural because they are completely unaware of the camera. Luck is important, however, since the photographer must depend on chance to bring his subjects close enough to light of sufficient strength to make photography possible even with a fast miniature camera lens.

Exciting fields of exploitation for the candid photographer

include crowds in front of theaters under brightly lighted marquees, well-lighted store windows and street scenes, market places and outdoor festivals at night under strong lights. A New York City professional photographer who specialized in candid pictures once made a series of quick snapshots, under festoons of colored light bulbs, of people's faces as they listened to a sentimental singer at a neighborhood-church street party.

Indoors, Leonard McCombe, famous *Life* photographer, who uses a miniature camera exclusively, works by the available artificial lighting, rejecting setup lamps or flash. However, he will help picture material along if he can do so without jeopardizing authenticity. If he sees a woman sitting at a table in a particularly interesting pose but in lighting that is not right, he will ask her to move a little and resume her conversation or whatever she is doing. He will then walk away and come back perhaps a half hour later and shoot his pictures without her knowledge.

Most amateur photography is done outdoors in good sunlight. Among the more advanced workers, it has come to be recognized that the soft light of early morning or of late afternoon is more agreeable than the comparatively harsh lighting of midday. One inveterate amateur has made it a habit for years to take most of his picture-hunting strolls about an hour after sunrise. At that time, he explained to me, the light is soft and has a fine atmospheric quality; nature is at her best; the city is just waking up to a new day; and the photographer, refreshed after a night's sleep, is most alert to impressions.

Although he prefers this soft lighting, he has been at the game long enough to know that lighting requirements vary and that, under some circumstances, other lighting will be more suitable. His usual routine is to take leisurely walks in different parts of town, examine details of light and viewpoint, and return later when conditions are right for the picture he wants. He notes the effects of lighting at various times of the day and at different times during the year. Some pictures take him days to get, some much longer.

This approach typifies the patient stalking of lighting effects by the advanced amateur, particularly the amateur of the old school. The latter was willing to wait; in fact, he saw no point in taking a picture unless the lighting revealed and described what he saw in the subject and what he thought about it. After all, was not lighting the essence of photography?

Ezra Stoller, successful New York architectural photographer, referring to the "very high standards" of seventy years ago, told me that in those days photographers actually used flat (frontal) lighting, today considered the mark of the rank amateur, to get full detail in the ornamental architecture then in vogue. "To get contrast," he said, "they developed to a lot of brilliance. They achieved depth through perspective rather than lighting itself. The results had to show each stone leaf and grain of stone, without black shadows anywhere."

Make Lighting "Fit"

Today's photographer looks with disdain at this use of lighting as suitable only for pure recording rather than for interpretation. He overlooks the fact that a type of lighting is by itself only an item in a catalogue of lighting effects; that *kinds* of lighting must be related to particular *needs* and that, under varying circumstances, the same subject may be lighted in many ways to say different things.

When we get to understand lighting, through much observation and much experimentation, we learn that even strong midday sun, which the rules say is always to be avoided, can reveal new meanings in subject matter.

It is not *always* desirable to have detail in shadows, such as we get under the diffused lighting of both ends of the day. Sometimes the strong contrasts resulting from the harsh light of noon tell us more. We should not take lighting for granted but should try to know it as a tool. Flat lighting, contrast lighting, full-scale lighting, all can be useful. Let us fit the lighting to what we want to say about the subject, avoid generalizations and fixed notions, and use lighting interpretively.

Because lighting is misunderstood, therefore misapplied, photographers employ filters indiscriminately. One photographer told me that while on vacation, he used a red filter all the time. He did so, he said, because the light was too strong. Was it not possible that a strong light was just what he needed for some particular subject? Did it not occur to him too that a red filter would give him too dark a sky and distort other values, so that his pictures would not be what he really wanted but substitute impressions?

He was allowing technique to rule his decisions; he was thinking of exposure for exposure's sake and not about the lighting effect it would produce. Reflecting a similar viewpoint was the injunction in an invitation to a camera trip to "bring plenty of filters," as one might say, "bring plenty of sandwiches or blankets."

A medium yellow filter will give almost any effect desired. Some photographers do not want even that much correction; Fritz Henle uses a light yellow, which is just enough to cut down the light intensity a little without changing light values appreciably. A photographer must understand what filters do, other than cut down the light and thereby call for an increase in exposure. When he puts the filter on the lens, he must be prepared for a change in tone values; he must be able to visualize the change and be sure that the new aspect of the subject is what he really wants.

Will a dark sky reveal something more important about the subject than you can say with a light sky? To what extent do you wish to separate the clouds from the sky, and do you understand that you can separate them more, or less, by the length of the camera exposure?

Light values are changed, too, when the source is diffused, and different effects are achieved under varying degrees of diffusion. Light clouds give a bright diffusion, result in soft shadows, perhaps a gay atmosphere. Heavy clouds make for almost shadowless effects and somber moods.

Light changes with the time of day, the season of the year, the state of the weather. The photographer should be careful to record the natural light values. When he alters them—through the use of filters, for example—he must first make sure he has a good reason for doing so, that the change is motivated by what he thinks and feels about the subject.

CHAPTER ELEVEN

Mood and Atmosphere

A mood is a state of mind. To exert influence in the desired direction, we must stimulate the observer's imagination.

ANDREAS FEININGER

MOOD IS THE "feel" of a place, of an incident, an occasion—the way *you* feel about it. The place, incident, occasion has no inherent feeling or mood; the mood is in you.

While you may agree that a place has grandeur, the mood it instills in you may vary from a feeling of awe to one of disdain because, perhaps, it may appear to you ostentatious. An atmosphere of simplicity or of quiet may give you the feeling of relaxation and restfulness; on the other hand, you may interpret the atmosphere as unreal for some reason and find yourself thoroughly annoyed, bored, perhaps resentful.

We say a place has "atmosphere"—grandeur, simplicity, quiet, or excitement—because on the basis of certain standards and life experiences most persons will agree that the given place has this or that attribute of atmosphere. How you *feel* about the place is something else again.

As a creative photographer, your concern is with the mood you feel, not with atmosphere as such. The one is your inter-

pretation of the subject; the other you try to record. Even
when the two coincide, your picture may differ from another
photographer's picture in the depth of feeling and insight you
have put into it.

A picture of atmosphere *only* may be a perfect rendering,
in all respects a technical gem, but while it may stir the observer to admiration for the photographer's skill, it may lack
the "something" that makes for emotional appreciation. We
tire eventually of merely "beautiful" pictures; they must make
us feel too.

Where the photographer introduces mood because he feels
strongly about the subject in a certain way, the picture comes
through to the observer with more or less impact, depending
on the photographer's technical skill and whether he has used
this skill intelligently to "speak his mind."

How do we say things about mood in terms of photography?

The way you say anything else in photography—through
lighting, camera viewpoint, and timing. You light the subject
to accent what you want to emphasize, subdue what you want
to keep in the background. You place your camera at such an
angle to the subject that the effect is what you want. And
where timing is a factor, as in the case of moving objects, you
wait until the components of the picture move into the places
you want them to be, then snap the shutter.

The more techniques you know, the more accurately you
will be able to record what you feel. But don't lean on techniques too heavily. Don't look for foolproof formulas on how
to get this or that result, how to portray a particular mood. The
techniques cannot tell you, specifically; all they can give you
is basic know-how to add to your photographic lexicon. Upon
this you draw as your needs dictate.

Saying Things with Techniques

Should you wish to photograph impressions rather than objects, you must learn to understand a basic premise: that techniques are words you can use to say similar things about very dissimilar subjects. For example, take the standard technique of a low camera viewpoint to state the idea of height. Using the very same technique you can interpret height in a tree, a house, or a person. Or suppose you want to say photographically that the subject is somber or sad. The same low-key, or "moody," lighting that you would use to light a bleak house on a lonely hill will do to describe a mysterious-looking street scene, the aftermath of a gay party, or a sultry glamour girl.

By the same token, if you wish to suggest movement in a photograph by deliberately using a shutter speed that is not fast enough to stop the most rapidly moving subject or part of the subject, you can say the same thing in a picture of flying leaves or birds, a performing dancer or athlete, a running horse or a moving vehicle, falling snow or a baseball moving through the air.

Take weather. There's a moody subject on which to try your technique lexicon. Overcast skies, rainy days, fog, or mist say different things than do good sunlight, open skies, and a clear atmosphere. Pictures taken in so-called "poor" light speak of an atmospheric quality that cannot be achieved in sunlight and that can turn ordinarily uninteresting ideas into story-telling photographs.

Ample opportunities for interpretations of mood are offered during the winter months. The amateur photographer, accustomed to summer field trips under a guide's leadership, may feel lost when winter puts him on his own. Rather than despair of finding subjects, he should accept the challenge to work things out for himself. He may discover, to his lasting advantage, that he does pretty well.

Winter picture material is far less obvious than the limitless range of subjects available in summer. Most amateurs see no pictures in winter unless the snow falls, but snow scenes are only one phase of winter photography. Deserted streets on cold days, the bared branches of trees in the park, the dark skies of bad winter weather offer chances to portray a mood-inspiring nature. Winter also has its gayer side, in the crispness and clarity of a cloudless, sunny afternoon, in the lively incidents of children at play, in the excitement of outdoor winter sports.

The photographer should try for results that give the feel of winter, the atmosphere of coldness. The best success is generally achieved with pictures of people engaged in familiar, everyday pursuits, in their attitudes as they walk against winter winds, plow through snowbanks, huddle against zero temperatures.

Pictures must have a "slant." Just as the writer emphasizes certain ideas to get his story across, so the photographer must choose the material, the approach, the lighting to drive home the point he is making. In his search for material, the photographer is aided partly by accidental discovery, chiefly by thinking out the importance of the event and how he can get this importance across in a picture. A snowbank can be photographed as just a snowbank or, with imagination, careful planning, and use of a dramatic point of view, as a snowbank of extraordinary proportions.

Many a photographer tries to include too much in the hope that somewhere among the details the observer will find the sum of the story he is telling. The better workers usually find they can be much more convincing, clear, and direct by closing in on some particularly dramatic detail, a small area which because of certain elements it contains sums up the story of an entire event—of a snowstorm unique in history, of a birthday party different from any other birthday party, of a wedding reception not quite like any other.

Get Mood, Then Keep It

You portray mood or depict atmosphere first with the techniques of the camera. You say as much as you can, drawing on all the pertinent know-how at your command. You say most of what you have to say when you take the picture, then put a period to your statement with a print. Don't depend on print manipulations to *manufacture* a mood for you. What you do not feel when you take the picture, you cannot really feel when you make the print.

Having taken the picture, you use appropriate techniques to make the film and the paper give you back what you saw and felt—and to the fullest extent of that seeing and that feeling. To this end, you employ whatever means may appear to you necessary; but be careful to reject any step you are tempted to use *merely* because that is the way it is usually done. A good many pictures in which the photographer has tried to show a mood do not quite come off for this very reason —that the mood was made to order, to fit a cliché mold. The picture *looks* artificial because it *is* artificial. Unless the photographer feels a genuine response to the subject, he cannot hope to put genuineness into his print, nor hope to impress the observer of the print afterward.

One of the most effective, as it is one of the most misused, methods by which the photographer reveals mood and atmosphere in a print is through diffusion, or softening of the image. Diffusion should not be resorted to merely because you like soft pictures but rather because the softness helps you to say something better than you could in a sharp picture. You should not overlook the fact that a sharp image may be more descriptive of the subject, as, for example, where you want to render texture or reproduce fine detail.

Diffusion is not used expressively when all you wish to do is to correct mechanical faults—as in the case of a "grainy" negative. Grain itself can add a kind of mood and is often used by a photographer to put across his intention. Photographers who have allowed their minds to be overburdened with techniques and who tend to work along established rather than original lines are too ready, too painstaking in their eagerness to correct such apparent "faults." Slight off-sharpness in a part of a picture, for instance, is not always a fault. Sometimes, as with image grain, it may be a contribution to the total meaning.

When they speak of "diffusion," photographers usually imply the use of a diffusing medium either in the camera when taking the picture or on the enlarger lens when making the print. A soft light—early-morning or late-afternoon daylight or, indoors, a light source with a screen over it—as a kind of diffusion, too, and should be considered by the photographer as the most direct means of getting the results he wants.

Try to do as much work as you possibly can at the time you take the picture. Limit your print making to getting the most out of your negative and printing paper in terms of story-telling tone values.

"Mood," or "atmosphere," is an over-all impression of a

scene or other subject. It may or may not involve the use of recognizable objects. It may be a play of light, a design, or other abstraction, yet the result may make us feel the emotion the photographer has tried to convey.

Abstractions

We are inclined to keep our noses too close to the ground, figuratively speaking. We frequently fail to see the forest for the trees—the immensity, breadth, and airiness of the open forest. We need to generalize more than we do in photography in order to gain a better perspective on what we are really after.

When we try to convey a feeling of some sort through abstractions, we create mood and atmosphere. The more we work in this vein, the better we are able to introduce feeling into a picture of objects, and the more readily our work is understood.

Mood and atmosphere are mediums of interpretation. They are the overtones in your picture, by which you communicate to the observer suggestions and connotations of meaning. Mood is that very personal element in a picture which is *you*—you saying something. When your picture lacks mood, it lacks you, your understanding of the subject, your special explanation of what the subject means.

Here is a familiar example: Take any well-known locale in your town. You pass it every day. Many other photographers pass it daily. But nobody takes a picture. One time you stop and look at it a bit. Something stops you. Is it the way the light hits it? Is it a strange figure in the scene you have not previously noticed because the light does not single it out? Is it something the rain has done to it, or the snow, or a chunk someone has knocked out of it somewhere to reveal something new about the subject?

Anyway, you take a picture, and because of the special way in which you see the subject, the picture has mood. You give it mood, the mood that is in you.

The mood of enthusiasm itself is the most important of all because without it the mind is sluggish and feelings are dormant. We see, feel, think strongly when we are most enthusiastic about something.

Enthusiasm is at its highest pitch when we work creatively —no matter how little our technical knowledge of the medium —when we discover things for ourselves, set our own moods, make our own interpretations.

CHAPTER TWELVE

Texture and Surface

The photographer is able . . . to depict with a fidelity having no parallel in the history of the arts, the full detail of a world replete with a limitless variety of visually satisfying textural forms.

HOWARD DEARSTYNE

ONE OF THE principal attributes of the photographic medium is the facility it affords for rendering textures and surfaces. Where other mediums call for painstaking copying by hand, the camera lens records mechanically and exactly what it sees. This is a great advantage, one so much admired by artists that they go to great lengths to imitate it. Indeed, an artist feels rather satisfied with himself when he has achieved perfection in this respect. Which is a bit like turning the tables, in view of the fact that many a photographer feels complimented when he is told his picture looks like a painting!

Despite this unique capacity of the camera for realistic portrayal of surfaces, photographers do not exploit it to the extent it deserves. Frequently, they ignore or debase it by failure to use the right type of lighting to reveal texture properly. In many instances, they deliberately destroy texture through processing manipulations designed to attain a pseudo-artistic result rather than photographic quality.

Texture is a component part of practically everything we photograph. Through lighting, we emphasize texture or merely suggest it. We may proclaim boldly, "Here is texture. Look at it. Isn't this wood splintery, or this old paint flaky, or this paper rough?" Or we may say, through less emphatic lighting, "Look at other things in this picture, but don't forget that the surfaces have texture too." Thus, although the photographer does not ignore the presence of texture, he alludes to it only casually.

The use of the texture-lighting technique in an emphatic way is not always appropriate or reasonable. It may, in fact, underline a detail meaninglessly, beyond its importance to the subject as a whole. It may be better to subdue texture, without ignoring it entirely, in order more effectively to get across the main idea of the picture.

When and where to put emphasis on texture, when and where to subdue it, is a personal decision which the photographer makes at the time he takes the picture. A blanket rule that such-and-such textured surfaces should *always* be revealed prominently and such-and-such should *always* be minimized may prove useful to the commercial photographer, who is hired to do a job according to specifications. It will never do, any more than will any other photographic rule, for the photographer who uses the camera interpretively to make personal statements based on his own responses.

The latter will usually point up texture when he employs it as the main theme in his picture or when he needs emphasis on texture as a supporting idea to the main theme. He will not use texture merely to display his skill in lighting and photographing textured surfaces—except as an exercise—but only to

render some meaning relating to the subject of which the surface is a part. Thus texture is used to say something about the
subject.

Put Life under the Texture

Texture by itself usually has no significance. The same or
similar texture patterns may be found on objects entirely unrelated to each other. Pure texture pictures will therefore be
merely puzzling, or at best belong in the category of "trick"
photography, in which interpretive meaning is seldom a factor.
When texture is associated with an object or a person, it assumes the vitality of a living thing. There is life under the texture, and the texture pulsates with the life that is under it.

Let us consider a few examples. The bark of an old tree,
for instance. What would you like to say about it? Realistically
show its age through strong side lighting or romanticize it by
using a more frontal lighting or make a generalization by
lighting it softly from the camera position? Sitting here, talking about it together thus, how can we tell? How can we
know here, away from the tree, in what way it is going to affect us, what mood it will inspire in us? The weather will have
something to do with our decision, the quality of the lighting,
how the tree is associated with its surroundings, and the need
that will be in us *at the time* to say this, that, or the other about
the tree.

Or take the ornamental ironwork in front of an old house.
The peeling rust of the one and the worn boards of the other
both offer subjects for application of the texture technique.
In both the mark of time is evidenced by texture, something
the imaginative photographer usually stresses. How much

stress? Again it depends on the individual photographer's viewpoint and mood. But certainly there can be no doubt that where texture is as expressive as in these cases, it requires sympathetic attention.

Photographers are too prone to treat this kind of subject in an oversentimentalized fashion and in doing so to obliterate texture almost entirely, substituting a false romanticism for the realities that tell us about the house. The rough texture of old boards and the scalings of rust on old ironwork can say much more than the thousand words reputed to be the worth of a picture. They speak not only of the passage of time but also of human experience and perhaps of former elegance. Where photographers ignore these values or do not even see them, they picture the subject not as it is but as something they "dreamed up." The creative photographer takes his inspiration from the subject itself. The noncreative, pseudo-romantic photographer superimposes an idea based on values that may have no relation to the subject.

Skin Textures Revealing

When we consider the texture in faces, we have something else again. Shall we reveal the wrinkles of old age any more than we show the imperfections in a young lady's face? You should answer this one for yourself, but while you are thinking about it, bear in mind the difference between imperfections in the young and signs of character in the old. Wrinkles are part of a subject's personal history and show the things that he is. Imperfections are just that and nothing more. But when you soften or smooth out wrinkles too much, by retouching, diffusion, or other means, you falsify your subject just as in the case of the romanticized old house and produce a substitute subject for the original, which is lost.

At the same time, skin texture can be exaggerated by the camera so that it is too pronounced. If we reproduce skin texture approximately as the eye sees it, the result usually will be satisfactory. Skin texture varies from the smoothness of babyhood to the wrinkles of age. The smoother the skin, the greater the technical problem involved. The conscientious photographer usually wants to show or suggest skin texture in some way. Other photographers find the rendering of skin texture too literal for purposes of interpretation, so they subdue or ignore textures altogether.

Photographers often feel justified in broadly suggesting the presence of texture in a subject without making any real attempt to use the texture-lighting technique. Texture does not always have to be seen to be felt. The photographer sometimes relies on the observer of his picture to supply, on the basis of his knowledge of the subject photographed, the unstated fact that the subject has texture.

Texture is an expression of intimacy. We have to get pretty close to look at it. How close must we get to put across our point? Must we narrow our camera viewpoint down to just the area with the most significant texture, or may we move the camera farther back so as to include more area and supply supporting data to the main texture theme? The procedure will vary, of course, depending on the part the texture surface plays in the complete picture and on how much the texture must be featured.

Due largely to its aspect of intimacy, texture usually creates an emotional reaction. We "feel" texture in a picture, and the more it is pronounced, the stronger is this sensuous response.

When we say the subject in a picture "looks so real you can almost touch it and feel it," we usually mean the texture has been rendered so well that it has the appearance of actuality.

Lighting Does It

The trick is in the lighting. Any photographer who cares to take the trouble—and all photographers must, as a matter of competence—can learn the principles, which are based chiefly on crosslighting of the subject, merely by working on the problem for a while. Often the task of becoming thoroughly acquainted with the use of light is undertaken in connection with the study of lighting nontextured surfaces. Edward Steichen is reputed to have photographed a white cup and saucer a thousand times in order to note the results of different lightings. Eugene Hutchinson, using a statuette brought back from France by his wife, tried hundreds of lighting manipulations in a similar effort to find out all he could about how light at different angles affected the texture and surface values of a given subject. Both photographers are masters of lighting principles and can get any result they need.

Textures and surfaces are intermingled in connotation. By "surface," we mean the face of an object, and by "texture," the structure of that face. Although all textures have depth and detail in some degree, not all surfaces are textured. Many are smooth and entirely free of a structural face. This basic difference makes a difference in the lighting techniques required. Surface lightings are comparatively simple to handle because the lighting angles are not so exacting, while the greater freedom of manipulation makes for the possibility of broader interpretations because minute textures are not involved in the picture's principal theme.

In rendering texture, the photographer is concerned with picking up detail. In the case of surfaces, he works with wide areas, sending the light across the surface in a broad sweep instead of at the very carefully adjusted angle needed for textural accent.

The difference between the two is reflected in the kind of pictures they inspire photographers to make. Because of the more or less close-up views called for in pictures featuring texture, these generally are more specific in their statements than pictures in which surface values predominate. The latter are in the main more adaptable to atmospheric treatment as, for example, where the photographer wishes to create a particular impression of the subject.

Photographers work to cultivate a sensitivity to the qualities of various surfaces and textures because they realize their dominant importance in the faithful rendering of photographic subjects. They know that only through a mastery of the techniques by which textures and surfaces are represented can they really make understandable comments about the subjects they photograph.

This slurring of technique unfortunately occurs frequently among so-called "documentary" photographers—just those workers who are most concerned with the problem of saying things in pictures. Freshness of approach, intent, and conviction are not enough; you need the technique to make them stick. Documentary workers are becoming more aware of their lacks in this connection, however. Those who are getting to the top in the field are climbing by dint of a growing mastery of all the techniques they need.

Texture and Technique

The lack of know-how in portraying texture may result in a picture in which the texture pattern is almost completely lost because of the wrong lighting. This is a frequent fault and is not serious if the photographer, having noticed that he missed the boat on one picture, tries to mend matters in the next. But when this fault is seen in picture after picture over a long period of time, then the matter can only be ascribed to lack of understanding of the importance of texture delineation where it is needed to tell the story—and perhaps even disdain the knowledge as being too limiting for creative purposes. However, the notion that imaginative photographers are necessarily sloppy technicians has long been outmoded. Today we expect the highest standards of our best workers.

Technique for expressive ends is no longer considered old-fashioned, as it used to be among some classes of photographers. It is definitely in the mode. The photographer who wants to get places had better board the band wagon, or he'll find himself far behind.

Creative photography is just a matter of seeing things from the right perspective, that is, from the idea *to* the techniques necessary to realize it in a photographic image. Not the other way about, which is stilted and impersonal. Photography of surface values gives us opportunities to use our imaginative faculty and test our skill.

For example, take a wet street just after a heavy rainfall. And suppose you want to photograph the idea of wetness— not merely the fact that the street is wet, but wetness itself. Instead of following the well-worn pattern of a view of the street, complete with sidewalk reflections, you may find you can tell a better story by isolating a section of the street or part of a wall, a rain-soaked fence, or perhaps just a very wet umbrella. By lighting and camera viewpoint, you can underline the idea of wetness through a close-up more descriptively than you could through a general view.

Since you are photographing an idea rather than an object, you can choose a wet window sill instead or photograph raindrops rolling down the surface of a window glass or maybe water being pumped from a well or the condensation of moisture on some surface.

Wetness is a surface quality, luminous and fluid and translucent. You may see it as gay or sad, a boon or a menace, refreshing or otherwise. Again, lighting, viewpoint, subject selection will state your case for you.

In a similar way, you can delineate a very dry surface, like a dusty sidewalk or the sheen of satin or the hardness and gleam of glass or the even surface of a rock smoothed down by time and the weather. A sense of atmosphere and a feeling for mood will help you raise your picture from the level of a mere record to the heights of interpretation, of how *you* see the cloth, glass, rock and what *you* feel and think about it.

Meanings in Surfaces, Not Surface Meanings

Appreciation of surface values results from awareness developed within the photographer. Look for these values and study them for meanings. Combine the wide-eyed curiosity and enthusiasm of the child with the sophistication of experience and the capacity of maturity to understand the human values that underlie surface appearances of subject matter.

Textures and surfaces have a language of their own. Their

language is the complex one of meanings. Hard to understand sometimes, easier at others. Meanings are clearest when you are feeling and thinking the most. You can translate this language into the language of photography which you know and thus become a sort of "interpreter" to tell people in photographs what the surfaces and textures are saying.

What do you photograph? Isn't it the texture or surface value as related to the object that attracts you and invites examination of its photographic possibilities? Surfaces and textures are the faces of the things you photograph. By their faces, as by the faces of people, you are made to feel certain responses and to form certain opinions about the objects. We say an orange has a "rough skin," an egg a "smooth shell," a walnut a "knobby surface," but we think of the *whole* object, not only of its surface characteristics; and we say an orange is "rough," an egg is "smooth," and a walnut is "knobby." The surface (as well as the shape—see Chapter 13, "Form and Shape") of the object becomes identified inseparably with the thing it covers, so that the knowledge we gain from the surface we translate in terms of the whole object.

Not all surfaces are thus translatable. Some are entities, like water, which can be interesting and informative by itself but whose meaning is subject to many variations. The previous example of rain showed that water can change meaning with every surface it falls upon. To the meaning of water as an abstraction, then, we add the realistic significance of its association with a windowpane, an umbrella, or wet boards.

When we think about surfaces and textures along these lines, we are moved by feeling too, not only about the surfaces and the textures as such but also about their relationship to other surfaces and textures and to life as a whole. Pretty soon things begin to hang together. They become interrelated in some over-all pattern, and the world starts to make sense.

When photographers learn to understand the world in this way, they form an individual philosophy about life and what they are doing in it and for it. And when they make pictures based on such a philosophy, they make pictures creatively.

CHAPTER THIRTEEN

Form and Shape

Someone with eyes keener than ours saw form in what we have passed by a thousand times. Someone has made uncommon, and very special, the common.

BEAUMONT NEWHALL

AN AMATEUR ONCE described a picture he took in these words:

"On the upper deck, looking over the railing, there was a young man with a straw hat. The shape of the hat was round. He was watching the men and women and children on the lower steerage deck . . . .

"A round straw hat, the funnel leaning left, the stairway leaning right, the white drawbridge with its railings made of circular chains—white suspenders crossing on the back of a man in the steerage below, round shapes of iron machinery, a mast cutting into the sky, making a triangular shape. I stood spellbound for a while. Could I photograph what I felt? I saw shapes related to each other, I saw a picture of shapes and underlying that the feeling I had about life . . . .

"I raced to the main stairway of the steamer; chased down to my cabin, got my Graflex, raced back again all out of breath, wondering whether the man with the straw hat had moved or not . . . . He hadn't moved. The man with crossed white suspenders showing his back, he, too, talking to a man, hadn't moved . . . . Seemingly no one had changed position.

"Would I get what I felt? Finally I released the shutter . . . . Had I gotten my picture? I knew if I had . . . here would be a picture based on related shapes and on the deepest human feeling, a step in my own evolution, a spontaneous discovery."

The amateur was Edward Stieglitz, speaking about his famous picture "The Steerage," which he took in 1907. I quote this because it expresses almost symbolically the elements of enthusiasm, inspiration, and imagination of the truly creative amateur. Elements that operate today, as they did over fifty years ago—and as they will fifty years hence.

Stieglitz spoke of shapes and the relationship of shapes as if they were components of a life drama, as for him they were.

If a photograph is to be more than a record—which, of course, it is inevitably when a photographer approaches subject matter in the spirit of a Stieglitz—then shapes, details, the materials of the image, are more meaningful than actual identification of the shapes. Still more useful to the creative photographer is the fact that these shapes relate in significant ways to tell a complete story.

When you run across a subject that appeals to you, it is the forms of the shapes that strike you first. Identification follows to explain them and give them added meaning. When identification is too forceful a factor—when, in a group, you are attracted first to one individual, then to another, and so on, without associating one with the other in some way—you don't see *a* picture but a group of pictures.

You must see a picture as one picture, all the elements of which are tied together to give you one general idea or impression. A still photograph seldom can do more than that and be effective.

I say this despite a picture I recall which might, at first glance, disprove my point. The picture, a news feature shot by Barney Cowherd, formerly of the *Courier-Journal and Louisville Times*, shows people standing at a street corner, apparently waiting for the traffic light to change. A subject which, if seen by a less sensitive photographer, might easily have fallen apart is bound together by the simple theme of isolation, each person preoccupied with his own thoughts and each seemingly not conscious of the presence of the others.

The picture was no accident. The photographer *waited* for this to happen, but because there was constant movement— people walking toward the corner—arrangement had to be on the wing. He had to see people as shapes rather than people as people, moving forms of shapes advancing toward the area that was his subject. When things "felt" right, when he saw the shapes related somehow, he snapped the shutter.

Press photographers often must work in this way. When things are happening fast, they watch for expressive forms, shapes that are doing things, saying things with body attitudes and with various movements relative to each other (for instance, a man swinging his body in a violent motion or in some other way disturbing an otherwise placid scene). The motion, the movement of the shape, catches the photographer's eye; identification follows. From his camera viewpoint, he thinks of the shape first—that will make the picture; the other will supply caption material.

How often have you encountered an incident and remarked, "There must be a picture here somewhere, but where is it? Everything is so confusing and separated from everything else. I wish the scene would pull together somehow."

Is It All Luck?

Maybe Stieglitz was lucky. Things were just right when he happened to look down at the crowded scene in the steerage. It was like a stage-set, but much better because it was real life. The people were real, and the situation was real. The relationship of the shapes heightened the reality and fused the details into a oneness that moved the photographer to trip the shutter—and that now moves us to appreciation of the resulting picture.

Maybe Cowherd was lucky too. But if he didn't have some kind of feeling for people, he would never have thought of the idea, certainly never have bothered to wait and wait on a street corner just to take a picture of people on the opposite corner. And if he hadn't waited and waited *feelingly*, he could not have seen the picture that finally took shape before his eyes— if the movement of the shapes had not provoked a responsiveness in him to people as people, men and women walking about in the world, each concerned with his own affairs yet bound to one another by the commonalty that is mankind.

We describe the form of shapes photographically by the use of light. Without light, shapes do not exist for the camera. Light rounds out shapes into spheres or squares them off as planes. Spheres and planes change in character with almost every change in the lighting.

The techniques are easily available in almost any manual, but the meaning *you* must supply through interpretation. The techniques are basic: light must come from the side rather than from the front in order to "model" the form of the shape you are photographing. Whether you are photographing planes or spheres, front light will give your subject the appearance of a disk rather than of a multisided or round object.

This is fundamental. Fairly simple too, isn't it? And yet, when you don't know what you are trying to say, you can easily become confused. You can make your square quite square and your sphere quite round, and that will be that. But the square or the sphere will not mean much of anything *until* you relate the two in some manner or relate each to other shapes.

The square has certain attributes the sphere does not have, and by relating the two to each other, you point up these differences and accent the squareness of the first and the roundness of the second. You may wish to oppose one against the other and, through lighting and arrangement, make the square or the sphere the dominant shape in your picture.

But mere dominance of one shape over other shapes is not the result you are after. You must make your point. For example, suppose you wish to interpret an idea of gracefulness. Your dominant shape will have some aspect of roundness. It will be curved and flowing and lyrical. In order to keep your idea from getting out of hand and to give it stability and a feeling of reality, you may find it useful to introduce square elements somewhere in the picture, or triangles or associated forms.

I do not mean by this that you necessarily *place* shapes where you want them, although you could do so, as in the case of still lifes (these do not have to be the lifeless things with which the term is usually associated—still lifes can come alive too). You relate shapes by vision, by selection of camera viewpoint, by an awareness of the meanings of shapes in a life incident.

Shape Connotations

Shapes offer meanings having to do with abstract ideas of solidity, of strength, of assurance, of the unyielding, the uncompromising, of the finite. They may also suggest notions opposite to these, such as weakness, indecision, fluidity, movement, the infinite. Shapes of the first kind are usually angular, regular; of the second, irregular, curvilinear, spherical. When you want to say things strongly, therefore, you choose the former and make them predominant in your pictures. For ideas of romance, beauty, elegance, femininity, softness, gaiety, you favor the latter.

Once you understand which shapes are characteristic of what, you know how to use them to the best advantage. But avoid rules. I, for one, certainly do not wish to give you the notion that while the shapes I have just mentioned refer to specific ideas, they are necessarily limited to those ideas. They are merely instances to help you build your own interpretations. A sphere, for example, may well make for an impression of boldness rather than one of yielding or indecision.

A good deal depends on the lighting, on the background, on the general atmosphere of the subject. Your treatment of shapes should reflect your thinking and feeling about the subject. Involve yourself with the subject emotionally; understand it emotionally; then interpret it with intelligence, with techniques calculated to make a statement that is complete and sufficiently clear to be understood by others.

The last is important. It is easy—and usually an admission

of ineptitude, whether conscious or unconscious—to say that
certain shapes mean something to you, and if others do not
understand, then it is just too bad. Instead, look at your picture objectively and try to find out where you *may* have
failed.

Shapes have to do with emotions as well as with ideas. Certain shapes have the power to make us feel fear, others to make
us happy or excited or depressed. The emotion may be due
to the form of the shape itself or to identification of the shape
with the subject proper. Thus, a highly grotesque masquerade
costume may inspire a degree of fear of the person wearing it,
even when it is known that the person is far from grotesque or
fearsome. The stooped form of a beggar may make us feel
pity; the shape of a gull in flight inspire a sense of grace or of
movement; the shape of a rocking chair may invite the feeling
of peace, suggest old age, or move us to nostalgic contemplation.

We are concerned with shapes when we photograph people
or animals or buildings or any other subjects having the
dimension of depth. We say we photograph this or that subject; we really photograph its shape, and the form or outline
of that shape inspires an idea, emotion, mood. In a portrait,
the shape of the subject involves the photographer in problems
of perspective, so that he does or does not distort the form; and
of camera angle, so that he does or does not exaggerate certain
features of the form, depending on what he is trying to do.

When we photograph groups, we are conscious of shapes
and "arrange" them so that they are related somehow. We arrange them in pyramids or triangles or some of the other
standard group poses. We try to fit them into a preconceived
pattern which too often is ordained by tradition.

Grouping

Eugene Hutchinson once showed me family groups he photographed in the early days of his long career. They were not arranged in an orderly pattern. I was amazed to see how a family group of as many as five, adults and children, seemed to "connect," even though I recognized no standard pattern within the group. The figures just "looked" right, and the result was charming and refreshing because it was natural. They looked as if they had just walked into the picture and sat down or stood around as they would normally. I saw similar work in the studio of Jane Reece, of Dayton, Ohio, a contemporary of Mr. Hutchinson, and realized that perhaps group posing was a lost art, a part of a way of life, of the temperament of an environment, that belongs to the past.

The photographer sensitive to the significance of shapes is able quickly to evaluate subject matter in formal terms. Attitudes, gestures, and movements reveal the characteristics of people and supply information about them. That is why Hutchinson and Reece achieved a naturalism in their groupings that make most of the studio-made group pictures of today look stiff and dull.

Shape relationship can give fresh meanings to familiar ideas. We don't look for subjects; we just find them. When our eyes are opened wide and our minds are alert, when the hearts within us feel, shapes unfold their meanings to us. It is not the mere *looking* for subject matter that brings results. It is the way we *see* what lies before our very eyes. Cultivate a way to see first; *then* look.

Shapes tell us what things are, so that even when we see it at a distance we can identify the subject by the form of its shape. Certain shapes are universal, like the characteristic shapes of a man, a woman, or a child, of a plow, a ship, a dwelling. Because such shapes have wide connotations, they are frequently used as symbols. In a given scene, the shape of a child may become a symbol of childhood; the shape of a dwelling, the symbol of all homes.

Symbolic, too, are the shapes of a table, a chair, a bottle, a pitcher, a lamp. We can use these shapes to make general statements about life or close in on specifics. The window of a store in New York's Greenwich Village which was being used by a "knitting circle" displayed two straight-backed chairs slightly inclined toward each other. I thought the display a wonderful example of how simple forms can be used to tell a familiar story.

Shapes are stationary, like buildings; itinerant, like vehicles; or mobile, like people. But none need ever be static. Even such highly flexible forms as the expressions on people's faces have been made to appear static in the hands of photographers without vision. On the other hand, a stationary object like an ordinary country house has been imbued with the vitality of a human dwelling, as in the work of Wright Morris in his book "The Inhabitants."

In the language of the photographer, shapes are "images"; but one will see them as static elements in an established pattern, while another will imbue them with meaning and life. Which kind of photographer are you? Which do you want to become?

CHAPTER FOURTEEN

Line and Pattern

I stand still or move slowly, feeling things like shapes, the direction of lines, the quality of surfaces. I frame with my eye (sometimes with my hands) as the ground glass would frame.

AARON SISKIND

MOOD AND ATMOSPHERE describe the "feel" of a picture. Texture and surface relate in more or less detail to the outsides of objects. Form and shape refer to the appearance, or body outline, of the objects. Line reduces shape to its simplest elements. And pattern links all together in the arrangement with which you make your photographic statement.

We see people's faces in lines as well as shapes. We speak of faces as "round" or "oval" or "square," etc., referring to lines rather than shapes, and we attribute to each certain characteristics. For example, we may say of the round face that it is "good-natured," "jovial," or "obese"; of the oval, that it is "graceful," "youthful," "elegant," "aristocratic"; of the square, that it is "rugged," "determined," "forceful."

With camera viewpoint and lighting, photographers emphasize an outline or attempt to minimize it in an effort to flatter the subject or to draw the eye away from the prominence of the outline, calling attention to something else they want to say about the subject.

Often the natural lines are altered. A scarf around a woman's head and face may make her round face look still more round or reduce it to an oval; her oval face, more oval and slimmer. Similarly, a hat on a man who normally goes hatless may supply lines that belie his character or give new information about him.

Lines tell us many things about people. The erect line speaks of self-confidence, of pride, arrogance, youth, strength; the bent line, of defeat, illness, age, of eagerness, absorption in a task. The curved line may suggest grace, activity, emotion.

As photographers, we learn to read lines and to interpret them in the camera. We use them in our pictures to reveal the character of an individual, or as in the case of a group scene, perhaps to convey the impression of an incident. But when we are preoccupied with picture formulas and techniques, our lines lack significance. They are mere exercises, even though the result may be offered as a complete picture, perhaps without our realizing that a picture is not complete until the photographer has given it meaning.

When photographers learn to understand the meanings implicit in the language of lines, then lines become a living lexicon capable of revealing the subtlest truths about people and things. Lines clarify details, accent a point here and there in a picture, add supporting data about the subject, and generally help to build individual images so that the result is an integrated and important message, delivered with impact.

Meanings in Straight Lines

Straight lines are vertical, diagonal, and horizontal and can be used to make simple or complex statements, either singly or in groups; groups of straight lines are parallel or diverging, varying or similar in length or height. Familiar examples of the vertical are the skyscraper, the country church steeple, the tree. We find the diagonal in the stairway, the hill, the roof gable. The horizon line in a seascape is the best-known example of the horizontal; the open plain, the bridge, the hedge are others.

The vertical is conventionally associated with ideas of dignity; the diagonal, with movement; the horizontal, with calm and finality. But such identification is only partially true. These lines, under varying circumstances, can mean many other things. We should not fix specific meanings to given lines but let them explain themselves when the time comes, that is, when we see them in subject matter, within the context of a given scene.

When a straight line is introduced in a scene containing curved objects, a feeling of stability may be established that was not there before and that gives the picture importance. Similarly, a scene containing many straight lines, which as a result has the feeling of monotony or coldness, may be softened in impact through the introduction of a single curved line or sphere in an appropriate place. Ordinarily, the interplay of straight and curved lines gives a picture greater interest and clarity than either one or the other used alone. However, there are wonderful exceptions. In addition, difference in the shapes and sizes of curves and in the lengths of lines may offer variety.

In groups, lines have added meanings. A notable example

is the "pile" of skyscrapers in lower Manhattan, which looks more impressive and attractive because the buildings are of unusual height and are dissimilar in outline than it would if they were all the same size.

We use lines to express ideas about places. For example, we may say the city is "vertical" and the country is "horizontal," because the tall buildings in the one emphasize the aspect of great height expressed by very high vertical lines, and the low structures characteristic of the country keep the lines down to "our size." When we call the city "vertical," we mean other things too, like the idea of confinement within the narrow streets and crowded sections of the metropolis. By using the term "horizontal" in describing the country, we may refer to the fact that people are allowed great freedom of space there, and partly because of this, lead a more leisurely and gracious existence than do city folk.

We can photograph impressions of these ideas and emphasize them by camera viewpoints based on our understanding of what lines do in a picture, what they say, and what they imply.

Cultivate a thoughtful curiosity about lines. Learn to search for meanings in them; get these meanings into your pictures. The lines are there in your subject, but unless you have learned to recognize them and to evaluate them for what they are worth to you in terms of their interpretive value, you will not be able to make the fullest use of them. You should learn to know lines not only intellectually but emotionally as well. You should not only understand values but sense values too. The ones you know and the ones you feel may be different, but the knowledge and the feeling are both important in helping you to make complete statements in your pictures.

Meanings in Curved Lines

The wonderfully expressive capacities of curving lines are illustrated in such familiar subjects as the flow and sweep of surf, the streamlined form of a modern ocean-going ship, the irregular line of a highway extending across hilly terrain. All spell movement. The photographer makes use of such lines to express or imply motion in the subject, and when he employs his technique effectively, he inspires the same sensation in the observer.

Curving lines are characteristic of the country and soften the outlines of the city. They describe the beauty of flowers and of foliage. They lend interest to the movement of dancers and of ice skaters and add to the excitement of an acrobatic performance.

These lines also help to stress the idea of perspective, of the recession of a scene or a series of objects toward some distant point, limited or infinite. In a well-made picture, they make the observer feel as if he were moving along too.

The curved line of the arch gives a graceful touch to a bridge, lends a feeling of sentiment to the doorway of a home. The circle is familiar in fruits, ornamental designs on buildings, party dining tables, children's games; it implies limitation, self-sufficiency, contentment. I have mentioned lines as they relate to people's faces. In addition to the human face, we find the oval in the oval-shaped dining table, the familiar egg, picture frames, throw rugs, and, in a modified version, in pears and other fruits.

We delight in watching the mobility of lines in the graceful routines of the ballet dancer, in the diagonal rows of marchers in close formation as seen from an upper-story window, in the curve of a diver's leap. Photographers frequently find interest in the diagonal and vertical lines described by the legs of people as they are walking, in the bent line of the fighter's flexed arm, in the stretched arm of the orator making a point, in the varied lines through which the skier moves down the ski run.

But you can supply many examples from your own experience. Did you make the most of your opportunities to photograph lines in each case?

Lines are woven into a pattern to make a picture reflecting the photographer's response to the subject. The pattern should never be set up by formula but should be an arrangement that binds together the subject elements in the way the photographer sees and understands them.

Lines merge with shapes in the final pattern, for lines are the simplified versions of shapes. All the lines we have been discussing assume shapes in the picture and should be represented as shapes. Through appropriate lighting and the choice of camera viewpoint, the line of the column is given roundness, the line of the tall building is given the dimensions of breadth and width; the "framing" lines of people's faces are filled out with the dimensions of life by using the same technical means.

The photographer may discover a pattern in an instant of casual seeing, as in a "candid" shot; he may construct it over a period of time (minutes, hours, or longer) by waiting for the elements to fall into place, as in action themes or where light of a particular quality is needed; or he may arrange it physically or by direction, as in still-life and flower photography. The latter approach has also been employed to give the effect of casual seeing.

"Seeing" Patterns

The more experience the photographer has and the keener his perceptions are, the quicker he is able to "see" meaningful patterns. He acquires, through an interest in what is going on about him and through a developed ability to "size up" situations, a sort of sixth sense of when and where to point his camera and release the shutter.

Ideally, the photographer should become deeply identified with the subject but at the same time retain a sufficiently objective attitude never to forget that he has a camera in his hands and wants to use it every significant moment. This ideal state can only rarely be attained, and then usually by the professional photographer, for whom operation of the camera is almost as instinctive as blinking an eyelash. But no matter what the approach may be, a deep and sympathetic interest in the subject, with a real desire to make an honest interpretation to the best of his ability, should be the motivation behind the work of every serious photographer.

The question of temperament must also be taken into account. A photographer may have a developed ability to see pictures, but because of the particular kind of person he is, picture taking "on the wing" may be out of his line. He needs more time for things to "shape up"—both in front of his camera and inside himself. The amateur photographer, to whom this book is primarily addressed, can *take* time—and should, if he needs it. Too often, the amateur shoots "anyway," just to see what will "come out," as if the camera possessed some magic quality to turn out pictures of its own devising.

Some photographers either dislike or lack the ability to "set up" a picture. Among these are the workers who prefer to photograph life as it is happening—living incidents, the face of nature in its various aspects—rather than simulate life in a pattern of their own making. They see their cameras as instruments for recording what they see, as nearly as they can, in the way they see it.

To my mind, they are wrong when they despise others who find they can say things about life more clearly and personally when they put together the parts of the picture pattern themselves. Many fine examples of this style of photography, notably in the experimental field, have been produced over the years, and more may be expected in the future. The approach calls for a comparatively high development of the imaginative faculty and some background in art.

But it is equally untrue to say, as it often is said, that only the second type of photographer is the creative worker and that those who photograph life as they find it are making mere records, objectively. It is the photographer's prerogative to work in the way he pleases and his needs require; no photographer or class of photographers has a monopoly on creativity. To whatever degree a photographer puts something of himself into a picture, by so much is he creative. The goal of creativity is great, but it takes little—just a bit of *you*—to attain it.

Shadow Patterns

Both the naturalistic and experimental photographer meet on common ground in the field of shadow patterns, which offers limitless scope for imaginative exploitation by all photographers. Shapes cast shadows, upon curved and flat surfaces as well as upon each other, thus creating more shapes, which vary according to the angle of the lighting, the nature of the surface, and the angle of the surface relative to the form of the original shape. These silhouetted, two-dimensional forms often have connotations and inspire ideas and emotions that intensify the meaning of the form from which they are derived. Sometimes they have significance of their own by reason of distortion or exaggeration.

The term "pattern" as used here, refers to any image or any combination of images assembled by the photographer in a meaningful relationship to make a complete picture of what he wants to say about the subject. The term does not apply in the literal sense of the conventional "shadow pattern," which has little value as an expression, or the "pattern" that results from a pointless arrangement of similar shapes, as a group of rowboats tied to shore or planks of lumber or a stack of barrels. The pattern I have in mind is the pattern of life, as visualized and represented in an imaginative and significant grouping of shapes by a thoughtful photographer. The term is analogous to "composition" (see Chapter 9, "What Holds It Together"), but there the similarity ends. "Composition," as ordinarily used in contemporary photography, has reference to fixed, ordained ideas of arrangement, whereas "pattern" is completely flexible and personal.

A line of people holding umbrellas photographed from an elevation may serve to illustrate. Because of the camera angle, one can hardly see the people for the umbrellas, and the group is so closely packed that the umbrellas seem almost to overlap. The picture is a warm human story, sympathetically told, and revealing a *pattern* of a life aspect. Yet the picture would hardly get by the composition clichés of the salons.

The candid portrait, picked out by a perceptive photographer in a street scene, can be commentary as well as likeness. Leon Levinstein saw opportunities for both in the character lines and details here.

A spot of light in the midst of a play of shadow forms comes as a surprise and accent in this moody abstraction by Harold Feinstein. Even so small an accent and in so simple a subject can be dramatic.

An attractive instance of the intelligent use of technique to create an effect. John H. Vondell picked the techniques of the close-up, depth of field, and framing to give us this unusual result.

Picture content sometimes dictates the format for the print, as in this nature composition by Giorgina Reid. Incidentally, even the traditional pictorialist cannot quarrel with this composition.

The lyric note is not seen too frequently in today's photography. This nature close-up by David Vestal is almost audible in the way the delicate values of detail, tone, and depth are communicated.

Like a Japanese print, yet essentially photographic, this shot by Kenji Ugaki achieves individuality through its odd calligraphy, the multiple pairing of subject and reflection to create a variety of design.

A mood of overpowering calm pervades this beautiful river scene. The gentle motion of the water created a pattern in tone, and the foreground and distant boats provided accent points and variety.

Photojournalism, and pictorialism at its best, are combined by Paul Berg of the St. Louis *Post-Dispatch* in this picture taken in the course of an extensive camera coverage of the Pescadores Islands.

Erwin Blumenfeld looked out of his hotel window in Paris one spring day and saw this sunny expression of the new season in a sprightly array of light and shade. It has a cheering, universal appeal.

CHAPTER FIFTEEN

A Moment in Time

The instant can be the end product of long experience as well as that of immediate surprise.

HENRI CARTIER-BRESSON

TWO PHOTOGRAPHERS take a picture.

One waits for a figure—any figure—to walk into an open space to fill a "composition," then trips the shutter, and walks away.

The other waits too, but his thinking goes something like this: "I need a figure in that space, but just any figure won't do. It must not merely fill the space but also give the space a meaning that is as yet incomplete. The figure will need to have a plausible reason for being there, will have to relate to the space in a significant way, and, above all, add something to it. His, hers, its appearance in that space must have sufficient importance to make the resulting picture a clear expression of what I want to say."

When the needed figure appears, the photographer trips the shutter.

That is "timing" in photography, in the true sense.

The other process is called "timing" too, but it is mechanical, thoughtless, and of doubtful value as a real expression. The first photographer merely fills space. The second photographer also fills the space, but in addition, he fills it with a new, a personal interpretation.

Timing is a two-way relationship between you and the subject, in which you bear the chief responsibility. Here is the sequence:

1. You become interested in a subject.
2. You make an effort to understand it.
3. As the result of your understanding of the subject, you reach certain conclusions about it.
4. You feel ready to say something about the subject in a photograph.
5. You say that something when the subject is ready too.

Interest

Interest would seem to be an obvious part of picture taking. But one has only to look in on a camera-club monthly competition to realize that interest in a given subject on the part of the members is not considered under the system of assignments prevailing in the clubs. The assignment idea may be useful in the classroom, where instruction is given in handling the subject and the work is part of the teaching routine. But in a competition, members are on their own, and if some are not interested in the assigned subject but participate anyway because of the incentive of scoring points, they are unfairly pitted against those who are interested and who perhaps have had some experience in photographing the subject.

By "interest," I mean genuine attraction to the material, leading to enthusiasm and a desire to know it better. Not the halfhearted approach of the amateur strolling through the park "in search" of material and snapping pictures now and then aimlessly. He is unhappy, and he is bored because nothing seems really to interest him. And very little will until he learns that he has to have more than just a camera to take pictures. In addition, he has to have a point of view and a curiosity about things to help him visualize his ideas. A real interest in the subject is the first important step in the process of picture taking.

Understanding

The second step is understanding. How can you know the right moment to take a picture unless you have a fairly clear idea of what the subject means and what you are after? When you are interested in a subject, you want to learn more about it. You dig below the surface values to the truth beneath. That way you get to know it intimately and are able to photograph it understandingly.

What do we mean by "understanding"? Let's get back to the park and try to find out. If we go to the park simply "looking for pictures," with only a vague idea of purpose, the pictures will elude us. But suppose we approach the park as the human theater it is, where everything we see is in some way associated with people and what people are, what they want, how they react in an atmosphere of relaxation. By studying yourself in relation to the park, you will get to know other people better because you will be impelled to identify yourself with them.

You cannot really get to understand people, in a park or elsewhere, until you have learned to understand yourself first. Basic principles apply to all humanity; what you learn about yourself you can relate to people in general and come out with similar answers. Self-knowledge helps you in photography, because when people laugh or cry, are relaxed or active, irritated or pleasant, indignant or amenable, you know how they must feel because you have had such experiences yourself on various occasions.

Understanding does not necessarily mean a technical knowledge of the subject. For example, you don't have to understand the engineering details of an automobile to appreciate its meaning as a factor in people's recreation. Understanding is interest, sympathy, curiosity, the human element of the equation. All kinds of automobiles, in conditions varying from pristine newness to near breakdown, take people to parks, to the seashore, across vacation highways, to everywhere.

What does it all mean in human terms? Does it help to know that a new car has the latest type of motor, which operates on such-and-such a principle, or that an old car's motor can be saved by a thorough overhaul job? This knowledge does not help you to understand the subject better, when the message you are trying to get across in your picture is the atmosphere of happiness and release of people on their way to play. Moreover, it is the promise of the relaxation and good times ahead that makes the folks in the shiny big car kin in spirit to those in the jalopy.

Understanding may result from an association of ideas. A subject ordinarily without interest or meaning by itself may acquire personal or universal significance through the connotations it evokes in the photographer because of something else he knows or remembers. Thus, a display of hard candies in old-fashioned glass jars may stir a feeling of nostalgia and inspire the photographer to take a picture rich in suggestion not only for himself but for others as well. The photographer may be affected in similar ways by a detail in the design of a house, a street scene lighted in a particular way, or a tree laden with fruit ready for picking, all of which subjects may give rise to childhood memories and the wish to recapture the atmosphere of earlier days.

Conclusions

Having come to understand the subject, we reach conclusions about it. We say this subject moves us to pity or hope, that one is beautiful or exciting, and so on. As the result of our understanding of the subject, we have a reaction, an opinion or feeling about it. On the basis of this reaction, we make pictures.

These reactions may change from time to time, and the changes may be reflected in the pictures you take. Many factors are involved in such changes: not only differences like variations in the weather and the lighting, which affect subject-matter interpretation to a very marked extent, but also differences in you. Whatever happens to you as a person affects you as a creative photographer. You make pictures differently this year than you did last year because of some experience—physical, emotional, mental—you have had in the interim, perhaps a new realization of the place photography has in your personal life.

The important thing is for the difference in you to be reflected in your pictures, for that way lies growth. The trouble with much of today's photography is that it does *not* reflect personal experience. Pictures continue to say the same old things in the same old ways when photographers make prints that have little connection with their daily living.

The final two steps in the five-step timing sequence listed at the start of this chapter involve the actual film exposure, for which the preceding three steps are a preparation. In practice, the sequence does not usually operate in this chronological order. Different photographers start at different steps in the sequence, yet arrive at equally important results.

You and the Subject

Having interest, understanding, and a viewpoint about the particular subject, you have what it takes, but are you ready yourself? The timing factor is both objective and subjective. The subjective aspect springs from your readiness to take a picture. The objective aspect is the subject's readiness to be photographed. Until and unless both you and the subject are ready for the picture-taking exposure, the timing will be off. You and the subject have to synchronize.

Let us break up the partnership for a bit. Let us take your situation first. You are ready to say something about the subject. You know the subject and have made up your mind what you think and feel about it, but the "how" of saying what you think and feel does not seem to be forthcoming. After all, you have a camera, not a brush, and you have to wait for things to happen in such a way that the subject reveals itself to you in its most significant aspects.

You may pass the subject daily for quite a while and look in vain. Things do not seem to click somehow. The spark is lacking. The special "something" is not there. It may be that the lack is in you, not in the subject. You may not be ready to take a picture because you have not developed your thinking about the subject to the point where it has specific meanings that can be photographed. Or perhaps a suitable mood is lacking. The subject does not "feel" right.

One day you see the subject as if for the first time. The "something special" is made apparent; your idea becomes crystallized. You know just what you need to make the picture complete and meaningful. Conditions do not happen to be right, that is, the subject is not "ready," but at least you know what you want. After that, it is a matter of waiting for the subject to "shape up" the picture for you.

I have elaborated this procedure in order to make clear the factors involved. Actually, the situation may take only a few minutes; but it may also take much longer. The point is that a two-way relationship does exist between the photographer and the subject, and when a picture is taken without regard for that relationship, the picture falls down somewhere. It misses fire because the photographer doesn't aim for anything.

When both the photographer and the subject are ready, when the subject communicates something to you, making itself as clear as possible through lighting, arrangement, etc., then timing is perfect. That is the moment when photography ideally takes place.

On the photographer's part, timing relates to mind and feeling; on the part of the subject, it is a question of many physical factors, of which lighting is one of the most important, in many cases *the* most important.

The photographer–subject relationship is illustrated by a series of candid pictures made by the late Dan Weiner, New York City photographer, during an Italian religious street celebration. Weiner knew the neighborhood and understood the people who lived in it, and besides, he was interested in people generally. His viewpoint was based on appreciation of the wholesome, genuine human qualities of the Italians and their love of holiday. He was particularly interested in the expressive qualities of their faces when listening to music.

Weaving in and out of the holiday crowd under the festoons of bright lights, Weiner was ready. He knew what he wanted: candid pictures of people's faces listening to the sentimental music they loved so well. The subject was naturally an extremely mobile one; it was "ready," but it was not easy to "pin it down" to an area which the photographer could aim at without his camera being seen. But Weiner got quite a harvest that night. The pictures had mood, pattern, and over-all significance. The pictures told about the people Weiner photographed, and they told about Weiner himself.

Element of Chance

A photograph in which everything seems to have fallen into place at exactly the right moment is often lightly dismissed as "just a lucky shot." Even when admired, the photographer receives only token credit for it, as if the picture had taken itself and the photographer had nothing to do with it.

But if this is true, one may well ask why some photographers score a high percentage of "lucky shots" while others seldom score at all. Instead of saying that some photographers are luckier than others, is it not more accurate to say that the lucky ones have certain qualities that help to make them that way?

The element of chance is inevitably present in all photography which attempts to record significant aspects of the passing scene. In fluid situations, objects, people, nature, and even the elements may move almost continually in their relationships to each other. As a result, a tiny change may make a big difference, a picture in fact where none existed the instant before.

Sheer luck is sometimes a factor, of course. The photographer just happens to be on the spot and ready when the event occurs and is within reasonable range of his camera. But in the main, the photographer is not merely lucky when he makes the shot; rather, he pushes his luck. Through training, observation, and the development of an alert attitude, the photographer learns to see, to evaluate, and to record his findings as if these three elements were one.

Alertness in photography is a combination of enthusiastic involvement in the situation being photographed and an excited readiness, or the mood of expectancy, not only for what may appear to be logical, but also for anything that may happen. Many photographers fail on both counts: because they have little real interest in the subject, they shoot it in a routine way; because they look for the expected, they miss the surprise twist and the picture.

The development of the ability, or rather sensitivity, to recognize in an instant the really important elements in any situation should be part of every photographer's training, whether for amateur or professional activity. This quality cannot be taught, of course, but it can be inspired and drawn out— by a sympathetic teacher, by looking at good pictures, by discussion with photographers, by listening to speakers who have something worthwhile to say. Under these influences, the serious photographer becomes increasingly aware of the smallest as of the most prominent details. Potentially, to him nothing is unimportant.

And always present are the possibilities of the accidental,

the unlooked-for but half-expected something. When it comes and the photographer shoots it, the picture may be called "lucky." Yes, the element of chance is present, a momentary revelation that comes and goes quickly. But who will see it and take a picture? The "lucky" one, of course, the photographer keenly receptive to the action, one who has trained himself to take nothing for granted and to be ready for the smallest change, to turn in any direction. Also, he is one who has made himself such a master of his craft that he works the camera instinctively. Vision is translated into camera action almost as rapidly as a muscular movement responding to a stimulus.

CHAPTER SIXTEEN

Color vs. Black and White

*Color can be imaginative and creative as soon as
both the artist and the public realize that color
does not have to be literal.*

ELIOT ELISOFON

COLOR PHOTOGRAPHY as a creative outlet is making considerable headway as photographers realize that it is not in competition with nor a replacement of black and white, but a distinctive
medium with its own values and possibilities.

"So many photographs—and paintings too, for that matter
—are just tinted black and whites," the late Edward Weston
said in *Modern Photography*. "The prejudice many photographers have against color photography comes from not thinking of color as form. You can say things with color that can't
be said in black and white."

In his color trials, he did not want to take the same pictures
he had taken in black and white, he said. "I wanted to think exclusively in color. As in black and white one learns to forget
color, so in color one must learn to forget black-and-white
forms. In spite of my early successes, I still didn't know much
about the technique, so I just followed the printed instructions.

You find a few subjects that can be expressed in either color or black and white. But you find more that can be said only through one of them. Many I photographed would be meaningless in black and white; the separation of forms is possible only because of the juxtaposition of colors . . . . Those who say that color will eventually replace black and white are talking nonsense. The two do not compete with each other. They are different means to different ends."

Color in photography can give mood or destroy it, Ben Rose, imaginative color photographer, told a camera club audience; it can be less realistic than black and white or it can intensify actuality.

It is paradoxical that whereas at photography's birth 130 years ago the lay public was disappointed that the daguerreotype did not show subjects in the colors of the original, black and white has become so much the accepted thing that color itself is often on the defensive. Life can look more real in black-and-white photography than in color.

In illustration, Mr. Rose showed a black-and-white picture he made in which the theme was the depressing one of delinquency. A girl was seated near a wall which in the original had a pinkish cast. Since this color is usually associated with a cheerful atmosphere, a color shot would have falsified the scene, he pointed out.

Color Disadvantages

Thus, color can be a distracting influence. Black and white can be more desirable, too, where line and design are the important elements. By introducing color in many such instances the design is often weakened because attention is lured from the design, which is the main reason for the picture, to the colors, which may be only incidental. Mr. Rose demonstrated that whereas color can help to identify the subject, this advantage may be questionable if it interferes with the impression the photographer has tried to convey.

However, color can be used both to accentuate shapes and to describe a mood. The use of simple colors, even monochrome, can be valuable in emphasizing form. Sometimes, moderate overexposure, resulting in an over-all airy quality, or even some unsharpness, can be useful in getting across a desired mood. Color can help to explain shapes and to identify objects and surfaces.

Color Variations

"You cannot tell with exactness what the color is going to look like anyway. A good deal of color work is accidental. You may aim for something, but you don't know the exact nature of the color you will get. Color results are unpredictable because color film emulsions today do not give fixed values. On different days, because of slight changes in light, the result from the same film may give you a little more blue, a little more pink."

Mr. Rose urged his amateur audience to work experimentally, to avoid "hamstringing your efforts with rules," to make pictures for themselves rather than for judges. Traditionalism is not always a bad thing, but it can be inhibiting and monotonous. Changing one's style occasionally will help to awaken new abilities, provide new fields to play around with, produce new and exciting results that appeal to emotions, stir responses in people. A picture does not have to be obvious. Mr.

Rose said that he likes the kind of picture that is intriguing, that first arouses a visual sensation, then invites him to figure it out."

Experimenting with Color

In similar vein, Edward Steichen, head of the department of photography at the Museum of Modern Art (New York), has said that the creative photographer is always experimenting, that every photograph he takes is an experiment. But unless the experimental attitude in photography is a full-time job, he adds, it is bound to be superficial. He criticizes the notion that experimental color is necessarily a kind of photography calling for a special approach; it is the attitude of a dedicated person, one who is constantly searching for new and more effective ways of communicating his visual impressions through pictures.

One cannot be an artist one day a week, turning the artistic sense on and off, he says; the serious photographer is involved in his art, and he exploits his capacities for creative work every time he takes a picture. True experimental photography, whether in color or black and white, is not concerned with trick effects, as is too often assumed. It is not the photographic manner nor the content that makes a color picture experimental, he feels, but rather the photographer's thoughtful, emotional, and artistic responsiveness to any material in terms of the color medium.

Many photographs taken in color could just as well, often better, have been photographed in black and white, Sol Libsohn, photographer and teacher, commented in the course of judging amateur color slides. "If you are going to take a color picture, you must have a reason for using color film, some color reason.

If color adds nothing to the picture, why not use black and white instead."

Color Criteria

His criteria in judging the entries were: "Does the subject compel the use of color; does the picture derive its appeal from the colors used and their relationships; what is the general color impression; does the color have a poetic quality?"

The colors need not be brilliant, he said; soft, weak colors that suggest atmosphere and mood sometimes are more appropriate and desirable than the literal rendition. In fact, film varies so much from one make to another that photographers in any event are obliged to learn what the differences are if they are to take advantage of them in making expressive pictures.

He made some general observations that apply to black and white as well as to color:

"I am not one of those who believes that you have to say something in a photograph; all I ask is that visually the picture should point up a specific idea," but "every photographer has to have an opinion, one that can be expressed visually in the picture he takes. People expect pictures to fall into categories; all I require is a good picture. As to composition, its only function is to help make the point of the picture."

He covered the major faults he encountered in amateur competitions. A recurring one was the lack of interpretation of the subject photographed: "The photographer failed to say something about the subject; it was not clear what he thought about it, or even what he had in mind. Others had too much in the pictures, indicating vagueness and indecision, or included elements that did not go together."

Color and Human Interest

Erwin Blumenfeld, *Vogue* color photographer, once chided his camera club audience for the relative lack of human interest in their "creative" color pictures, reminding them that there is much more to life than the stone walls, houses, doors, etc. which they seemed to favor. He was not aware that in amateur circles the term creative has been so distorted that club members have become conditioned to thinking in terms of color patterns, design, and effects rather than any kind of visual experience.

Mr. Blumenfeld compared the color slides with the members' black-and-white prints, which showed a real interest in people and were more imaginative than the color efforts. In color, photographers take nature too much for granted, he said, and on the whole do not feel as much involved with their material as in their black-and-white work; personality fails to come through as frequently.

"My first impression of the slides was that the show consisted mainly of reflections and examples of construction. I was astonished to see so many pictures and so few that dealt with people."

Mastery of Color

Color photography has been made so easy for the man in the street that many amateur photographers, and some professionals too, who feel handicapped in black-and-white photography without a fair mastery of the medium blithely tackle color with no more than box-camera knowledge. The steady improvement in color materials and the fact that adherence to color lighting and exposure instructions almost invariably assure pictures that "come out" has encouraged indiscriminate shooting.

The sight of mere color, without regard for harmonious relationships of hues which can come only through understanding of color essentials, appears to be adequate justification for color pictures. Moreover, even where a more serious attitude exists, the tendency is to rely on "intuitive" feeling for color and to avoid the disciplines of the medium on the ground that they inhibit "creativeness." As in black-and-white photography, where a similar situation has existed for some time, an adequate grounding in the principles involved certainly leads to a higher level of output.

You are the one new and unique thing in your environment. The newest thing is you.

HELEN MILIUS

Part 3
New Patterns . . .

CHAPTER SEVENTEEN

New Patterns for Learning

You are a slightly different person from having heard this program from what you were 55 minutes ago, and I am also a slightly different person than I was 55 minutes ago from having given it.

DAVID RANDOLPH

TEACHING IS A cooperative effort. My wife, who has been alternately student and teacher most of her life, tells me that teaching is two parts learning and one part teaching. "What the teacher does," she says, "is to set in motion a process of learning, a process in which the teacher often changes place with the student. His principal function is to create an atmosphere in which learning occurs."

The creative teacher soon realizes that a flow of ideas from only one direction, rather than a two-way relationship with students, must soon empty the teacher and discourage the class. In photography, this one-way flow has led to a general tendency for students to mistrust their own inclinations and to rely on their teachers for direction.

The result, so widely prevalent among photographers, is dependence on the ideas of others, or imitativeness. Because the emphasis is merely on the transfer of information from a source (the teacher) to a passive recipient (the student), the relationship between the two becomes static.

Most teaching in commercial schools is geared to turn out photographers on the principle of the assembly line. This is held to be justified by the fact that commercial photography is largely a matter of pleasing a customer or creating desire for a product, thereby leaving the photographer little scope for individuality.

But when this regimentation appears in schools whose primary purpose it is to teach the expressive aspects of photography, such as the many classes and schools for amateurs, the time has come to call for a change. We require a new kind of schooling, in which enlightened teachers understand the need people have to communicate their thinking in some way. Given enough such teachers, we could effectively counteract the present stultifying influence of those who offer their students no more than techniques as mechanical, inflexible tools for the propagation of ideas belonging to others.

Every teacher of photography who is really interested in his student's development as a creative photographer (the term "creative" is used here in the sense of an individual speaking for himself, not echoing somebody else), must eventually come to the conclusion, if he does not start with it, that a student begins first as a person, then articulates as a photographer.

Everybody has something to say, a something colored by his background—the place where he lives, the way he spends his leisure time, the manner in which he earns his living, the people who inhabit his daily existence. The more complete the person is, with respect to his capacity to understand and to feel, the greater will be the variety of his experiences and the depth of his responses.

"What sort of person is my student?" the teacher should ask himself. "What does he need in the way of guidance, and how much can he take in at a time?"

Such knowledge is not easy to get. It is particularly slow work at first, the chief problem being to build the student's confidence in the teacher's sincerity to help him progress. The teacher leads, but he should also inspire self-reliance and independent thinking. He should "draw out" the student rather than impose his own knowledge on him; encourage the student to use whatever capacities he has, right from the start, to say things in pictures, however imperfectly.

It Works Both Ways

The real teacher does not set himself apart from his student, as one handing knowledge *down*, but acts as one sharing with another what he knows and hoping for a return in kind. The teacher who insists on the attitude "Do as *I* do and say; never mind what *you* think!" not only short-changes the student of his just expectations but loses a chance to add to his own development.

The helpful teacher soon finds himself in a way "involved" with the student in a mutual effort to reach solutions to problems, both interpretive and technical. In the process, if the search for an answer is sincere and thorough, both student and teacher contribute: the one, with questions about what he is trying to say, the other, with suggestions to help the student clarify his thinking. This working together gives both a mutual interest in the result. The student moves forward as a photographer; the teacher improves his capacity to teach creatively.

The insistence on quick results has hampered this kind of approach to teaching even where competent teachers are available. How soon after he begins a course can the student be expected to work creatively? In a sense, putting aside the problem of differences in personality, if we consider the camera merely as an extension of vision, he can start immediately, although his pictures will be incomplete due to lack of technical knowledge and competence.

Most students, however, will need a great deal of help in their initial efforts and may not be able to achieve real expression for some time. Since learning is an individual process, it is impossible for the teacher to predict accurately where a particular student will be at the end of a course. In fact, even students with real creative potentialities may not be able to show distinctive prints until some time after the end of the course, until they have worked by themselves for a while.

Grossman's Approach

The kind of teaching I have been discussing is best embodied in the philosophy and instruction methods of the late Sid Grossman, who demonstrated a remarkable ability to put students on the road to meaningful work in photography. His approach survives in the teaching philosophy and method of some of his students and colleagues.

The student begins with an attempt to answer the question "What is my function as a photographer?" The instructor helps him by pointing out that his photographic work is not shut off from the rest of his life, that photography is itself an act of living, a way of increasing his knowledge of the world, of seeing old things in new shapes and with new meanings.

"The basic aim" of his teaching, Grossman pointed out, "is to help the student to develop a personal approach to photography; to understand the limitations and potentialities of the medium, to learn to make his individual interpretations of his immediate world in terms of a progressively broadening understanding of the medium.

"The student is taught to appreciate the photographic medium for its unique qualities, such as the ability to catch the fleeting moment; the characteristic of the camera to make a statement of maximum plausibility; the camera's capacity to delineate textures and realities of materials, water, and sunshine, with a minute quality of definition not possible with any other medium."

The teaching approach starts the student off with the barest minimum of technique necessary to manipulate a camera, develop negatives, and make contact prints. The student learns technique as he needs it. As his experiences in photography present new problems to him, he learns the technique necessary to solve these particular problems. To this end the instructor tries to suggest experimentation calculated to lead students to provocative problems. Grossman felt that a student gets more out of an explanation of why he failed to get a result he wanted in a picture than he does from a lecture before he makes the shot.

"We give each student only what he needs in technique and advice," Grossman said. "Where he goes from there is his own business. He has to understand the material he is photographing and to use this knowledge in picturing the moods and movements of people. Every good photographer develops a special idea of life. We urge our students to work in this direction and to do something fresh; to be creative, wide awake, and to use initiative."

Unique Approach

A philosophy of teaching that has for its main goal the tapping of whatever latent capacities the student may possess and putting them to work on a creative level is the practice at the Institute of Design in Chicago's Illinois Institute of Technology. The school's attitude is that potentially "everyone is creative" and that its principal function is to help the student to bring this quality to the surface in productive ways.

Its approach to the problem is exploratory and experimental. Often considerably handicapped by a student's previous conditioning of poor teaching and environmental influences, the school's instructors have the double task of "peeling off the petals" of conventional ways of seeing and thinking of their students and at the same time striving to free them for new ways based on the discovery and use of unrealized abilities.

In addition to training students for a career in photography, the school also offers training for professions in visual design, equipment design, shelter design, and building research. Placing emphasis on the development of the ability to visualize creatively, unhampered by habit and prejudice, rather than on the merely technical, the school starts all students, regardless of their chosen profession, in the basic foundation course.

This takes a year and a half, during which the student learns to become familiar with the nature of materials, how they respond to handling, and various ways of using them. Thus, he experiments with wood, clay, wire, paper, etc., learning not only how they behave under a variety of treatments but at the same time breaking down familiar thinking in terms of the material itself, and gradually introducing the concept of working in terms of what can be done to make the materials yield something new.

For the student photographer this training in visualization gives him appreciation of the look and feel of materials, textures, forms, etc., and the opportunity to shake his mind loose of ordinary ideas and to think along original lines.

"In time," says Aaron Siskind, instructor, "it is expected that the student will begin to sense something going on within him that he had not previously experienced—an urge toward, and discovered capacity for, creative effort. When this happens he is ready to start working in photography for the balance of the four-year course, during which we teach him how to exploit and use his newly found talents through the medium of the camera."

With the stress on photographic seeing, the beginning photographer–student gets a minimum of technique, no more than he needs for the job in hand. He is told about photosensitive materials and how they react to light, the basic phenomenon being illustrated with photograms, then takes up the camera. He learns how to focus and is told what the needed exposure should be; he picks up techniques as he goes along. For example, when in working on a project he comes to such a problem as depth of field, the instructor takes time out to explain, but with only enough data to make it possible for the student to achieve his purpose.

Similarly, the student learns how light works on objects as seen through a camera, how it describes form through light and shade, surface and texture, reflection and refraction, density and transparency. He works in black and white and in color with still and motion-picture cameras, or with combinations of the two plus other graphic mediums.

Since the four-year course, a combination of visual and mechanical training, leads to the degree of B.S., it includes also a general education, with such courses as English, history, etc. in the full curriculum.

Contest Reveals Quality of Teaching

The role of the teacher and supervisor in the photographic activities of junior and senior high school students was clearly reflected in many of the Scholastic-Ansco Photography Awards entries in a recent judging. The prints submitted to this annual competition by young people throughout the United States indicated in many instances the supervisors' ignorance of photography, inability to develop or inspire the student's potentialities, and, frequently, an attitude of indifference to the student's interest in camera work.

These faults were the more glaring when the results were compared with those achieved in photographs whose makers apparently had the benefit of intelligent, conscientious, and capable teaching. In such instances, the prints were outstanding not only in terms of meaningful and attractive images but, in the main, also in craftsmanship.

The bad teaching was evidenced by many entries that obviously should never have been approved by the instructors for entry in the competition. Other pictures showed signs of having started with an idea that had photographic possibilities but that failed of achievement because of an instructor's incapacity for or unconcern with the student's efforts.

That poor teaching and guidance were at the core of the unsatisfactory results as a whole was the fairly unanimous opinion of the jury of several judges. The judges looked for ideas, originality, spontaneous responses to material, honest impressions. Technique was a secondary factor in the evaluation; frequently the judges gave high awards to poor prints and rejected others which were better photographed and printed but were barren of meaning.

Many of the pictures showed a striving by the young exhibitors honestly to interpret what they saw. In these efforts they proved that youthfulness is no deterrent to mature thinking in photography, as judges sometimes declare, but that poor teaching can keep the results of such thinking from coming to the fore.

Student's Role

Little can be achieved, least of all development of the student's individuality, without his full participation and, to some extent, initiative, plus a real desire to learn. But since it is true that despite this cooperation on the student's part, he is frequently led to imitate rather than to express his personality, can it be that the teacher unwittingly—for example, by disapproving of some pictures while approving of others—turns guidance of the student's own ideas into direction along group lines based on the instructor's ideas? Individuality can also be discouraged by the teacher's manner, in which he may actually dictate an approach, though intending only to suggest or to illustrate it.

In view of the pressure on all sides toward conformity and a standardized product, it is not surprising that teachers too have some difficulty in carrying out their objectives. But it is side-stepping the issue to say, as some teachers do, "Our job is to teach the techniques and nothing else." The truly creative teacher interprets his responsibility differently. He realizes that he has an unparalleled opportunity to give the student the wherewithal, in terms of training and thinking, to fight the conformity to which he will inevitably be subject when he goes out on his own.

The teacher's greatest responsibility—and this is particularly true since the teacher himself is so acutely aware of it in the educational field generally—is to initiate new patterns of learning, patterns which recognize development of a personal approach as the prime objective. For where outside of school can the student find an equal chance for stimulation along creative lines? Where better than in school can he "try his wings" without having them singed by the flames of experience? The demands to conform to standards, to fall into line with one or another of the established patterns, to select a particular groove instead of forging his own way—all these exert their pressure too soon.

It has been my own experience that students frequently have been so conditioned as mere recipients of information that they disparage attempts to involve them creatively in the learning process. They want information handed to them literally, pre-digested, complete, and unalterable. This attitude makes the creative teacher's job much harder, of course, but at the same time it offers a wonderful challenge: he must strive to prepare his students for a new kind of learning. Unless the teacher meets this challenge squarely, he will not only be remiss in his responsibilities to the student but will himself be pushed back into the sterile old ways of lecturing, with the student following uncritically. The result will be just another photographer who makes pictures like everybody else does instead of a personality who makes pictures that reflect himself.

By its very nature, the prevailing lecture system in teaching photography promotes thinking along group, rather than individual, lines. The system assumes, both from the standpoint of the student and the instructor, that all wisdom lies in the experience and the mind of the teacher.

Learning Together

Photography is too personal merely to be "taught" in this manner. Even where the student, accustomed to the same kind of "learning" in other fields, demands it, the teacher must take leadership in a more creative direction. As I have said before, rather than hand down information, he should invite the student to join with him in the cooperative venture of learning together, of searching together, town-meeting fashion, for the answers to the student's problems of personal expression.

This cooperation is best promoted in a class through group discussions in which the teacher participates only as a leader. Thus, the student will be taught not merely to receive but to weigh, to question, to clarify for himself and to adjust knowledge to the needs of his own personality.

He will learn that photography can be a personal thing, the techniques of which must be interpreted individually, not accepted verbatim. To develop this approach, the student should be encouraged to ask at every turn, "What does this mean to me? How can I use it to say what I want to say in pictures?"

The prevailing atmosphere of the class will then be such

that every student will in effect be "discovering" photography for himself. And with this sense of discovery will come the enthusiasm and the stimulus without which creative photography is not possible.

CHAPTER EIGHTEEN

Lessons at Exhibits

*The purpose of photography is the transmission
of a visualized sector of life through the medium
of the camera into a mental process that starts
with the photographer's thinking about the subject he photographs and is continued in the mind
of the spectator.*

DR. ROMAN VISHNIAC

TOLERANCE OF THE other fellow's viewpoint will do more to
help photography "go places" than any other single factor.
Photographers who live in mental birdcages, deliberately shut-
ting themselves off from outside influences, must inevitably
become artistically sterile; their pictures, repetitious and lifeless;
their thinking, sluggish and uninspired.

The photographer with a progressive outlook, that is, an
open mind to other approaches than his own, invariably scores
gains for his personal development. The benefits accrue chiefly
as the result of observing the work of others sympathetically,
of making sincere attempts to understand what they are trying
to do in their pictures.

He will find some values "good," some "bad." Some photographers will offer him nothing, while others may open his eyes to ways of seeing so fresh and meaningful that they amount to mental massages, stirring his imagination, revealing new worlds of mind and spirit.

Leave your yardstick at home when going to exhibitions. Give the other man a chance to get his message across to you without having to conform to your personal notions of photographic standards. Don't go to an exhibition with a chip on your shoulder, daring the exhibitor to persuade you to change your ways, particularly when you know the pictures will be of a type radically different from your own. Maybe he will; maybe he won't. The greatest value of an exhibit lies in its power to help you, another photographer, to understand more deeply your own approach, to sharpen your perceptions, to give them a new insight and intensity.

Steichen's Exhibits

I know of no exhibits of photographs where the photographer can learn more, get more stimulus for his own work, and see the photographic medium from so many new perspectives as he can at those of Edward Steichen, director of the Photography Department at New York's famous Museum of Modern Art and dean of American photographers.

These shows have given a new meaning and vitality to the word "exhibition" and demonstrate a formula for photographic appreciation and effectiveness that becomes more convincing with each succeeding one. The "formula" gradually unfolds as show after show, "exploring tendencies, techniques, and directions in today's photography," reveals the master plan: not only to display photographs by competent photographers but to offer, in effect, a "course" in self-expression, designed to influence constructively the work of all serious photographers who take the trouble to study them carefully.

A group of three of Steichen's "little shows" will illustrate how he contrives to instruct and inspire at the same time, purely by means of example.

The first show demonstrated how three photographers observed and interpreted different human situations. Steichen said he based the show on the "assignment" idea because he felt that the value of a photographer's work was best revealed in how well he discharged a given task.

The photographers were Leonard McCombe, who showed a series of pictures of displaced persons in Europe; Wayne Miller, who was represented by a group of close-ups of his wife's face as she was giving birth to their son; and Homer Page, whose pictures were candid shots taken during an American Legion convention.

McCombe, a leader in the realistic style of vital human portrayal, showed how people look and act in the face of an uncertain future and when bowed down by recent personal tragedy. Miller's record extended beyond the limitations of a personal experience because of its universal implications. And Page's candid glimpses were cutting commentaries on human behavior.

The second show displayed the work of six photographers on the single theme "Music and Musicians."

Three of the photographers, in search of a way to interpret Yehudi Menuhin, the violinist, arrived at three separate answers. Yousuf Karsh's Menuhin was boyish, a bit self-conscious and posed, but confident. Philippe Halsman's was the mature musician—dignified, formal, absorbed during a performance.

Adrian Siegel caught Menuhin in a candid moment during a rehearsal, depicting the violinist as just another working artist anxious to do a good job. Of the three, Siegel's photograph, though technically the least worthy, was probably the most human, understandable, and sympathetic.

The different treatments were equally characteristic of the approach of these photographers to other subjects. Just as the three remaining photographers represented at the show—Gjon Mili, W. Eugene Smith, and Fred Plaut—displayed their individual styles.

As in the case of Menuhin, Halsman's portrait of Marian Anderson dignified the subject as a great artist, emphasizing the interpretation by a low-camera, three-quarter-figure viewpoint. Karsh's treatment of the same subject relied on posing, lighting, and expressive mood to portray the singer's personality rather than her artistry.

Pictures of Listening

An interesting comparison of the photographers' diverse ability to see similar material was revealed in the pictures of conductors and musicians listening to music. Although Smith, Siegel, and Plaut all used the same technical facilities—35mm miniature cameras and the normal lighting of the concert hall and recording studio—Plaut was content to photograph the atmosphere of listening rather than the listeners themselves; Smith's approach was to make listening a living experience, revealing character as well as mood; in similar vein was Siegel's "listening portrait" of Arturo Toscanini, in which the conductor seemed to be transported into the world of music.

That this picture was not merely a chance shot but the

result of thought and understanding on the photographer's part was shown in another of Siegel's Toscanini series. The conductor, leading his orchestra, was photographed against a dark background, only the upper part of his body showing. The effect was that of a spirit hovering above the musicians, not directing so much as inspiring their playing.

Steichen's third show reflected four ways of thinking photographically as revealed in the work of four photographers having widely different points of view.

The photographers were Lisette Model, Bill Brandt, Harry Callahan, and Ted Croner, each one strongly individual, each with a different style, each with something on his mind. Steichen could hardly have picked a more diversified group: the critical Model, straightforward and sharp-cutting in her characterizations; the moody Brandt, deep in thought, almost impressionistic; the introspective Callahan, who abstracts from real objects the essence of their meaning for him in terms of pattern, texture, and design; the youthfully exuberant Croner, who breaks technical rules to reveal his unbounded delight in the excitement of city life.

The chief lesson of the show lay in these very differences and in the proof offered by the pictures of the extreme flexibility of the medium to express markedly individual ways of thinking and feeling.

The show was dramatic as well as instructive. The comparisons were almost startling, but the point was made clear to the thoughtful observer that whether the photographic language be monosyllabic, as in Model's tart comments, or almost obscure, as in Callahan's abstractions, pictures can be such real expressions that something from each adds to the sum of your own efforts as a creative photographer.

To get the most out of such a show, however, requires a tolerance on the part of the observer-photographer that unfortunately is far less evident today than it should be. We tend to eye with suspicion, or to dislike, any photographer's work that differs from our own in over-all approach or technique.

The four-man show taught that this is nonsense, that the only real criterion is the photographer's honesty, not the manner in which he elects to have his say about life. Because they express themselves so definitely, in such individual ways, you know that Model could no more "speak" in the manner of Brandt than could Croner work in Callahan's direction. And vice versa all around.

It is not a question of which is the better. When two photographers work in similar fashion, then you can say, "I like this man's way better than the other's." But how are you going to compare unlikes—as in this show? The best you can do is to evaluate each on his own merits and decide that, within the limits of his approach to material, he has been successful or not; that within those limits he has been convincing or ineffectual.

Similarly, the question is not whether you agree with this or that one's approach but whether each photographer succeeds in getting across to you the atmosphere of the truth as he sees it. If the photographers can make you feel, understand, or even guess at something they are trying to do, that is the most you can expect.

Let's see how it works out. You ask yourself, "Do these photographers tell me things I did not know? Or, if I did know them, are they said in such a way that my knowledge is deeper and has more meaning than before?"

Varied Viewpoints

I asked myself this question as I surveyed the separate viewpoints displayed on the four walls of the intimate little room reserved for these exhibits. I tried to disregard subject matter and consider the characteristic style revealed in the work of each photographer. The fact that I liked Brandt's work the best of all, because I found it the most congenial, because it moved me deeply, did not, however, prevent me from being exhilarated by Model's revelations of human character. From the one I gained a new appreciation of the subtlety of values; from the other, a new interpretation of the strength and conviction of the direct statement.

Although Callahan's work touched me less, yet I could see how a preoccupation with hidden meanings could give a man comfort in a confusing world. By reducing life to pattern and design as he has done, he achieves for himself a feeling of comparative security, of orderliness and plan beneath the apparent chaos.

With Croner's pictures my emotions swung clear out to the surface of things again. Here was excitement, boyish enjoyment. Here no subtlety, no brooding, no comment, but pure delight with life. Everything was wonderful—and no questions asked.

A comprehensive survey of contemporary photography was demonstrated by Steichen in a large show of about three hundred prints by more than sixty photographers, the now-famous "In and Out of Focus" exhibit.

To illustrate how different workers approach similar material, the theme used by Steichen in the little shows, the pictures were arranged in groups. Thus, movement, portraits, city impressions were grouped separately. The pictures in each category were so arranged as to complement each other and were integrated to support, intensify, and clarify the main theme.

An outstanding feature of the show was the range of individual expression it revealed. This was due largely to real attempts on the part of the photographers, many of whom were amateurs, to say things convincingly because they felt strongly. Since the motivation for making the pictures lay in an intelligently emotional response to the material, the results were often original, never static or standardized.

The value of the show was not in the use of technique as such but in how the technique was employed as the vehicle for an idea about something. The pictures mirrored states of mind, individual ways of seeing, straightforward reactions to subject matter. The photographers used only such techniques as were necessary to record their impressions and no more.

On the whole, the exhibition was a well-rounded survey of current trends among creative photographers. These trends were summarized in the implication of the show that the photographer who wants to do *real work* must cater to his own instincts and feelings about material, respond honestly to what he sees, copy no one, and please only himself. The amateur was encouraged by the fact that much of the material was familiar and ordinary, well within his everyday experience.

Although the Steichen exhibits referred to here are among his first few shows at the Museum of Modern Art, they will suffice to illustrate a phase of his goals as exhibition director, namely, to teach through pictures alone and by comparing examples. This is the only aspect of his work that is pertinent to the theme of this chapter.

In succeeding and the more recent shows, he has placed

more emphasis on the diversity of photographic aims and achievements. In a few memorable instances he has employed photography as a vehicle to project an idea rather than to show what photographers have done and are doing on a creative level.

Of these, his 1955 "The Family of Man," an extensive display of photographs from various parts of the world on the theme that people are basically alike in their needs and relationships regardless of where they live, set a record for attendance at the museum and is still attracting huge crowds as it makes the rounds of large cities in various parts of the world. It offers, incidentally, remarkably brilliant and effective proof of photography's power as a means of communication on a universal level.

CHAPTER NINETEEN

Picking the Winners

*A top-notch pictorial photograph . . . must
"do something" to the observer.*

CHARLES A. KINSLEY

ANY EVALUATION OF the pictures that win prizes, that are
selected for hanging in exhibitions, or get recognition of some
kind as the result of a competition with others, cannot be made
intelligently without knowing these facts:

1. Who submitted the pictures?
2. Who made the selections?
3. What was the predominant standard of the entries
   as a group?

For example, if the contributors lack ideas, imagination,
and the ability to make effective photographs, and the standard
of the group is, as a result, quite low, the pictures selected
must be a choice based on the principle of the lesser evil. The
"best" pictures will still be bad pictures. They will merely be
slightly less objectionable than the others.

On the other hand, if the judges have a narrow viewpoint
and stick to their preconceptions of "good" photography,
closing their minds to anything that runs counter to their arbi-

trary formulas, then even an imaginative contributor has little chance of winning. Which brings up the point that judges—of pictorial salons, in particular—have both the responsibility and the opportunity to encourage fresh approaches to subject matter. And those who do not see it that way or consistently prove that they do not, from the pictures they turn down, should not be invited to sit on juries.

The censure, then, that falls on such judges, must be shared, at least in part, by the club or exhibition committee that chooses them in the first place. It is up to the committee to pick the judges most likely to make a fair and constructive appraisal of the prints that will be set before them. Of course, we could keep on in this vein and examine the qualifications of the committee itself.

There I would stop, however, for I believe that the character of the "powers that be" in any club, group, or association of photographers influences the photographic thinking of the membership of that group as a whole.

Rochester International Salon Survey

The quality of a judge's thinking and his attitude toward photography are important factors in any effort to raise the standards of camera work where judges are called in to select "the best" and discard "the bad." A survey along these lines made one year by the Rochester International Salon should be useful, because the show included a variety of photographic work—press and documentary, pictorial, nature, and color. In effect, the committee asked the judges what they expected of the pictures they were going to evaluate and the basis on which they would select or reject.

The replies were instructive, particularly in view of the diversity of approach.

Roy E. Stryker, of the press and documentary jury, assumed good technique, pictures well organized "in relation to the purpose which the photographer has in mind when he takes the picture." His prime consideration was that the documentary pictures be "interesting and authentic records of significant subject matter."

On the same jury, the publisher, William L. Chenery, relied on journalistic standards. "As a journalist," he said, "I would imagine journalistic standards would certainly be applied to press photographs and also to those classed as 'documentary.' The editor of a newspaper or magazine selects both photographs and text on his judgment of their interest first and of their significance or importance second. The journalist assumes technical competence and honesty. These are very general qualities, but in journalism I have always thought too precise rules more of an embarrassment than an aid. I certainly would not wish to exclude anything which seemed to be honest, technically competent, interesting, and important even though it came outside the familiar categories."

Paul Threlfall, newspaperman, looked first for "impact" in documentaries—the feeling and emotional effect a photograph has upon an individual. Photographic quality was also very important, in his opinion, but he implied that he would not penalize a photograph merely for lack of quality; that if the impact is strong enough, he would be inclined to overlook faults in printing.

He said further, "The feeling of the strenuous efforts necessary in the making of photographs—picturing myself in the shoes of the photographer who made the picture, how the picture was made, and if it appears that it might have been possible to have done better with a little more ingenuity—might be somewhat of a factor in the selection of a prize-winning picture. Many pictures that are outstanding and contest material, though lacking in quality due to conditions that no photographer could overcome, should certainly be given every consideration."

In the pictorial class, J. H. Vondell, successful pictorialist, saw the salon picture as consisting of subject, composition, and print quality. He wanted to know first, "Does the picture say something? Does it show imagination or quick thinking?" Composition consists in "filling the picture space pleasingly and interestingly," and print quality "is simply common-sense selection and use of printing materials."

Nicholas Haz, teacher of photography, expressed a preference for the standard techniques but was open to persuasion when departures from the rules produced a well-motivated result. He reflected the tendency of judges to tolerate bad subject matter if the technique is admirable: "If the subject is trite, perfect technique and composition are demanded. If the subject is original, humorous, inspiring, or otherwise thrilling, then small mistakes of technique and image arrangement are forgiven." However, "evidence of hard labor in the making is not considered a virtue," he said, "just the opposite. The light touch, seemingly effortless work rates high with me."

In the color class, H. J. Johnson wanted pictures that were "coherent in intellectual or emotional story, whether representational or nonrepresentational in subject material. Print or color quality can be considered as practically prerequisite."

O. E. Romig expected a good color slide to have good composition of subject matter and color; be more than a record;

tell a story, say something, evidence personal artistic feeling or mood; show originality in theme or execution.

Charles A. Kinsley looked first for good technique; second, for evidence of feeling, some reason for making the picture; third, for simplicity in arrangement and harmony of the colors. "Finally, and most important of all," he felt, "a top-notch pictorial photograph must have an emotional effect on the observer. It may be admiration, happiness, sorrow, excitement, anticipation, envy, or any other effect—but it must 'do something' to the observer."

In nature photography, an added factor is the need to render a scientific fact with accuracy. The judges in this class were Edwin Way Teale, a specialist in the field, Mrs. Matthew R. Barcellona, and H. Lou Gibson.

Mr. Teale said he judged a nature photograph, "first, as a photograph (technical); second, as picture (lighting, viewpoint, composition); third, what meaning has it?"

"The best nature photographs," he elaborated, are those which, after fulfilling the first two considerations, "possess a third important feature. They tell a story, reveal something of interest or importance about the subject. Thus a picture that has recorded some activity or development in the life of the subject is a step ahead of one that merely records a sharp picture of the subject, other things being equal."

Mrs. Barcellona listed four standards:

1. Interest. What story does it tell or what scientific fact does it illustrate? How well does it do this?

2. Composition. How well has the photographer utilized these elements to make his picture effective?

3. Difficulty of shot. Naturally, the harder a shot is to get, the higher the rating.

4. Quality. Is the photographer master of his camera and of his darkroom facilities?

Mr. Gibson held that "in a nature print the clarity with which the characteristics of the subject are shown is the only first requirement," though "of course, artistic and technical qualities are added up too." "A nature print," he explained, "should be such that one who knows the subject need not look at the title. And one who has never seen the subject before should be able to recognize it after seeing the print."

Ideas Preferred

Thus, it appears from their own statements that certain judges not only look for ideas in pictures and for evidence of real feeling but may even close their eyes to small technical inadequacies in the presence of a notable attempt to communicate a real emotion or other message. I am inclined to believe that, in the main, photographers are more at fault, for reasons discussed elsewhere in this book, than are those to whom they show their work in the hope of approval.

Miss Dorothy Grafly, reporting "On Being a Juror," pointed to a similar situation in the art field. Her comments fit the situation in photography so aptly that they could as well be applied to picture making with a camera as to painting.

She remarked that although the particular jury on which she served required "from each artist a certain originality of viewpoint and ability to handle materials," they invariably had to reject entries for these very reasons, namely, "poor craftsmanship, imitation, and lack of individual viewpoint."

There was also a familiar ring for photographers to such of her statements as: "Obviously an appalling number of the artists submitting were going, not to nature, but to the work of other artists, and were trying to reproduce the surface of what they saw there."

And: "Even more discouraging was the dead level of mediocrity in composition that should never have been submitted."

And: "What concerned us more than the level of mediocrity was the fact that any number of art students apparently had been given so little critical basis for judging their own work that they considered it ready to submit to a professional jury."

Photographic salon committees which insist that the jury select the number of prints required to fill a given exhibition space, even when there are not that many acceptable prints among the entries, should ponder the fact that the jury on which Miss Grafly served had the courage to reject all but nineteen of 923 submissions. Unfortunately for photography, such strict insistence on high standards and such unwillingness to make compromises is not known in print salons.

Artists on the Jury

An experiment in Baltimore, Md., to demonstrate, at least by implication, that artists are better fitted than conventional salon juries to judge pictorial exhibitions resulted in little that was conclusive but much that was helpful as to standards. However, it raised serious questions as to the feasibility of the new method. The occasion was the judging of the Baltimore International Salon of Photography by a jury of three artists, Harry Sternberg of New York; Benton Spruance of Philadelphia, and Jacob Kainen, curator of graphic arts at the Smithsonian Institution.

Mexican children peering through a school window made a bouquet of young faces for Sonja Bullaty's camera. The face nearest the camera is the key image, the other faces suggest the environment.

When a photographer has become sufficiently a master of his craft, he may depart occasionally from the "rules" to try effects, as in this blurred (slow shutter) shot of a skating couple by Allan Blynd.

Sam Falk of *The New York Times Magazine* used the selective focus technique to sum up a picture story on teen-age delinquency. Key effects are the powerful silhouette and the abstraction of the background figures.

Lawrence Siegel's candid eye had to move unobtrusively and warily to record this situation—the sense of loneliness and self-absorption. The effect is heightened by the presence of other figures in the picture.

A masterful example of alertness, plus some luck (the middle and distant figures are "placed" just right), this description of opulence can hardly be surpassed. The picture was taken by Inge Morath.

Robert Doisneau is unexcelled among photographers for his unique ability to find humor in the most ordinary subjects. Small though they are, the key figures here are the lovers in the street, almost outside the picture.

An air of mystery and intrigue appears to surround these tall figures conversing earnestly on a Paris street corner. Typical of the French photographer Brassaï, the picture has an awe-inspiring effect.

The photographer's big problem in shooting a subject with constantly changing elements is to spot a pattern quickly enough to catch it in the lens. K. Yuzuyama has succeeded handsomely in this exciting shot.

228

The artist jury had been selected by the museum in place of the usual pictorial salon jury as a condition for allowing the use of its walls for the annual salon. The previous year, the museum had barred the show, which until then had been an annual event sponsored by the Baltimore club, on the ground that salon pictures are "monotonous and repetitious."

The judging was one of the strangest in salon history. Here were three artists so completely unaware of salon clichés that they frequently threw out without a second glance some of the "best names" in pictorialism, so free of salon traditionalism that they were neither impressed by print quality nor dismayed by the lack of it. The small audience of pictorialists who watched the proceedings were by turn aghast, confused, and mildly annoyed as print after print which by all the "rules" should have not failed, fell by the wayside, and as many prints were accepted which should by the usual yardstick have been promptly rejected.

The holocaust was great and disastrous as many fond pictorial shibboleths suffered the ordeal by artist jury. Out went the nudes and the flowers, the "studio night" portraits, the cute animals and cuter babies, and the sentimental landscapes. Print titles were "superfluous," one judge remarked, so they were never read. Nor were the judges any kinder to pretentiously contrived "creative" pictures submitted obviously in the hope that they would please an artist jury.

The audience for a long time had difficulty in following the artists' reasoning, but gradually it became fairly clear that they looked for good design and arrangement, were intrigued by texture, mood, and atmosphere, and were moved by picture content, the photographer's sincerity and ingenuity.

Summed up, it would appear that the experiment was successful in that, in their innocence of salon thinking, the artists judged on the whole a picture's total effect, its power to hold the observer's attention by communicating a deeply felt statement. This attitude is new, refreshing, and progressive in salon judging. A weakness of the judging was developed in the tendency to evaluate prints in painters' terms, to look for painters' qualities in the prints, and to lack real appreciation of the photographic medium itself.

Thanks to the excellence of the jury, the experiment was a positive and fruitful start toward better standards in salon exhibitions. The next step was to find jurors who combine the high caliber of taste, judgment, and artistic acumen of these artists with a sound knowledge of the photographic medium and recognition of its potentials.

Money as an Incentive

What is the situation where the incentive for entering better pictures in competitions is a large sum of money rather than space in an important show or the gold medals and ribbons of the salons?

Surprising as it may seem, the incentive for better work is quite small in the prize-money contests, which, on the contrary, present a striking paradox: that despite the "big money" offered by the sponsors, the contests serve only to perpetuate mediocre achievement.

A. Aubrey Bodine, the winner of the top prize in an international contest conducted by *Popular Photography*, believes that "prize contests offering high rewards are tremendously important because they supply a strong incentive for photographers to make better pictures." The incentive is there, of course (everybody likes money), but the facts of the contest in which he came out on top do not bear out the hopeful note in his statement. The contest seemed, instead, to attract some of the most insipid examples of the salonist's "art"—with the usual few exceptions. But these are unfortunately but a drop in the bucket in a contest where as many as 90,000 prints are submitted!

One must reach the conclusion, then, that the better photographers do not participate in money contests in sufficiently large numbers to make their influence felt. And why not?

Philippe Halsman, noted magazine photographer, gives a partial answer. "Professionals are afraid to compete because of the fear of losing out to inferior photographers" on a basis of the judging that substitutes other values for the top standards of the craft. Of course, all competent photographers should be included in this statement, whether of professional or amateur status.

Perhaps the principal reason why more good photographers do not compete is the fact that recognition is largely a matter of chance. Whereas a really fine photograph is almost certain to be hung in a high-caliber exhibition, the same print may lose out in a contest to a picture by a novice who happened to get a "lucky shot."

Despite all this, I agree with Bodine. The incentive of large cash prizes is both a wholesome one and powerfully attractive. I would like to see more good photographers drop their dignity, be sporting (if that's what it takes), and get in there and compete with their best pictures.

Win or lose, they are bound to raise the general quality of contest entries to a level of respectability and achievement these competitions do not now enjoy. And that is a contribution they should be proud to make.

CHAPTER TWENTY

A New Deal for the Camera Clubs

Pretty pictures are only an escape from the subject. Photography is a statement; it has to tell us things about the subject.

BERENICE ABBOTT

CAMERA CLUBS HAVE been under fire for years on two fronts. One is the articulate and condemning attitude of progressive photographers, who see no hope for improvement and believe the clubs should be ignored as a factor in American photography. The other, equally destructive but inarticulate, manifests itself in a negative approach to the clubs by the members themselves.

Since the first is intolerant and offers no solutions, we may safely forget it. I am more concerned with the causes for apathy among the members. I recognize the many weaknesses of camera clubs, which have contributed to this attitude. At the same time, I am inclined toward optimism, for I see too much evidence of dissatisfaction to believe that club members will not change once they are helped to find the way.

True, this is happening only in scattered instances, with an individual here and there. The change, therefore, may come very slowly and sporadically. There may be frequent backslidings, and only the hardy may be able to weather the bludgeonings of pressure to stand by the clichés. But a start will have been made, which may in time have the effect of vitalizing entire clubs into more purposeful photographic activity.

What *is* wrong with the camera clubs? It is understood, of course, that nothing will be achieved toward their improvement until the clubs realize that lacks do exist. For to know "there's something wrong" is part of the battle, since this admission immediately opens the mind to the possibility of help in new ideas. Otherwise, the clubs will be in exactly the same position as the critics who see no good in camera clubs at all and therefore believe it futile to offer suggestions for betterment —even if they can think of any.

To begin with, it seems to me that camera clubs will not progress a single step until they recognize the premise that conformity with the established standards is wrong and that individuality must be noticed and encouraged. Progressive groups within camera clubs whose leadership insists on the *status quo* have this alternative: to start new clubs in which the desired aim is introduced as the basic premise, namely, that photography is not merely the product of film, paper, and developer, duly processed, but the communication of ideas and honest feelings.

Pictorialism Rules Clubs

Camera clubs throughout the country are ruled almost without exception by pictorial thinking. This makes for a deadly sameness of approach from coast to coast and an intolerance of any viewpoint that does not fit in with the traditional standards. The first step to camera-club betterment, therefore, would be to encourage members to make any kind of pictures they like and to assure them of a fair hearing. Since pictorial-minded photographers, for example, would in the main be incapable of evaluating so-called "documentary" work with sufficient objectivity, commentators with broad photographic viewpoints would have to be called in to do the job.

The rubber-stamp similarity of the camera clubs shows up very markedly in gatherings of groups of clubs. What happens in the individual camera clubs also happens at the group meetings, only more of the same and involving a great many more persons. Nothing is learned because nothing is contributed, and the photographers return to their respective clubs no wiser or more inspired than they were before. Little is done to help amateurs move forward.

Poor Leadership

The second great weakness of the clubs is the poor leadership. In most cases this is composed of the "elder statesmen" among the members, that is, members who have achieved some renown in the salons and whose opinions and examples therefore are held in the highest esteem by the rank and file of the club. Leadership has thus become almost dynastic in character and is looked to on every occasion for guidance concerning picture-making standards.

Since individuality in the truly personal sense of the term is generally frowned upon in the clubs, this "guidance" is passed on and accepted whole, just as the present givers got it from those who preceded them. For that is the nature of the pictorial hierarchy, and that is the way it will continue to be until challenged. The challenge will come most effectively from club members themselves, once they realize the unwholesome restrictions and aimlessness of contemporary salon pictorialism and assume a critical attitude toward their leadership, based on a compelling need to produce pictures more expressive of their own feelings rather than "ready-to-wear" impressions manufactured for them by pictorialist tradition.

The third major weakness of the camera clubs is the lack of, and the need for, an atmosphere in which creative capacities can flow. Attempts should be made to dispel the fear of making pictures different from the "accepted standards" and to encourage experimentation in new directions. It should be recognized that members often do have ideas of their own but lack the self-confidence to carry them through; that, as a result, they distort or vitiate their ideas for the sake of the "standards" in order to win acceptance among their fellow members and success in the competitions and exhibitions.

Although clubs ostensibly are organized for the purpose of exchanging ideas among members and for the mutual benefits that should accrue in an association of persons with a common interest, these ideals are realized only in limited fashion. The intended spirit of mutual helpfulness is restricted to an exchange of formulas, of chitchat about point scorings in competitions, and other equally trite information.

Discussion Needed

The club's greatest opportunity, that of making the most of an association of persons of different backgrounds and with varied experiences and ways of thinking, is largely wasted.

Hardly any attempt is made to facilitate free discussion of ideas rather than mere techniques and to help members compare notes so that each can learn something of the others' attitudes toward picture making.

Thus, opportunities are cast aside that, if properly directed within each club, could be one of the most constructive factors in giving the "lift" they so sorely need. This is a big job for somebody—and that somebody is a composite of the president, as chairman of the meetings, of the program director, who picks the visiting speakers, and of the print director and his committee, who handle the competitions and club exhibits.

The first can go on announcing chitchat signifying nothing and stop there, as he usually does, or he can turn the meeting into something worthwhile by introducing discussion along lines intended to help the members find themselves as creative photographers.

The program director can do his job better by exercising more discrimination in the selection of guest lecturers and by organizing programs calculated to help members help themselves. Speakers should be selected who can make real contributions to the sum of the members' knowledge and ability to think along creative lines, not merely say the same old things in the same old ways and leave members exactly where they were before. Better to have no speaker at all than one who wastes the club's time in this way.

The print director has, in a way, the greatest responsibility, for his selection of judges and types of club competitions can influence members for better or for worse. The way he handles these matters can mean the difference between progress within the club or stagnation; there is no middle ground.

Take the monthly club competitions, for example. Members are assigned a subject: "Portraits" one month, "Table Tops" another, and so on. Having been assigned a subject, the members are thereafter left to shift for themselves. But what is a club for, if not to help its members? Granted that photographers should make their own pictures and not be led by the hand, for an individual approach should be the aim of every serious photographer . . . . Still, where a competition is concerned, it seems to me that every member should be given an equal opportunity with his fellows through a briefing on the essentials of this or that type of subject. The individual approach will come through in the way each photographer sees and handles the material.

A case in point is my experience as judge of a camera-club competition on "Architecture." I gave first prize to a print which showed a corner of an old structure highlighted by a spot of late-afternoon sunlight. This treatment of the subject, which conveyed the feeling of old stone and the atmosphere of age that characterized the building, revealed a sympathetic understanding of the essentials involved. The other entries, however, showed that the photographers had completely misunderstood the assigned subject.

This fault was due largely to lack of interest, which came out in the common tendency among the pictures to evade the subject of architecture and to stress other features. In one picture, a snow mound in the foreground was so emphasized that the architecture became secondary. In others, human figures were introduced in an effort to supply interest, but each attempt invariably was a failure because the architectural subject itself was mishandled. The photographers seemed, in many instances, to be more intent on supplying a figure than on trying for a strong arrangement of the subject matter. The architecture thus became incidental, and since the figure appeared to have no other function than to fill an open space, the result was pointless.

This competition again pointed up the question of whether assigned subjects in camera-club tests really serve any purpose other than to supply material for scoring points. Perhaps a far wiser and more productive program would result if the members were allowed to bring in their best pictures in any category. The photographers would then make only the pictures they wanted to make, and since in that case there would at least be the incentive of personal interest, the general level of the entries might be raised.

Choice of Judges

The print director's second serious responsibility is in his choice of judges. This part of the job will become easier as pictures become better, as photographers work to a personal standard rather than base their efforts on the narrow premise of salon acceptability. Although we still have many old-line judges, who deny recognition to all prints that ignore the "rules" because the photographers try to think for themselves, such judges may easily be identified and their prejudices become known. The progressive print director will avoid them and will select only those who, when the available prints give them the opportunity, show a real desire to favor pictures having imagination, feeling, and individuality.

The Club Meeting

The "main event" in camera-club relations remains the periodic meeting, which is the president's responsibility. This is a much harder task, when conscientiously assumed, than it appears to be from the manner in which it is often handled. On the face of it, all the president needs to do as chairman is to open the meeting, read a few announcements about such matters as dues, perhaps introduce a speaker, and close the meeting.

Actually, his job is the much bigger one of exploiting the talent and viewpoint of each member for the general good. To this end, he must use his power as chairman to minimize discussions about technical trivialities and the petty bickerings that arise when members lack interest and direction.

He will do the membership the greatest service if he turns discussion of techniques into such instructive channels as the uses for the techniques in helping photographers to realize thoughtful aims. He will help members to help each other if he draws them out in group talks to tell of their experiences in trying to get ideas across in their pictures. He should try to get them to say where they failed and where they succeeded and to explain as well as they can the reasons in each case. He should try to involve other members in the discussion, so that all may make whatever contribution they can to the topic in hand. Thus, all will become personally concerned, and all will be helped, because most photographic problems have universal application.

Sharing by Members

Camera clubs attract members of varied intelligence, sensibilities, and artistic talent. People join camera clubs because they like the idea of pursuing a common avocation in the company of fellow enthusiasts. Many are eager to share with the less gifted the benefits of comparatively superior background and advantages. For example, a member who has had some art training will not hesitate to fill out another member's deficiencies in this respect; on the other hand, the artist will seek and expect to receive information from a member who has experience and talent in fields of which he himself is ignorant.

But such sharing seldom happens by itself in the competitive environment prevailing in most clubs. It comes out in the atmosphere of mutual helpfulness and intelligent discussion that a meeting chairman can set in motion. If the president does not see this function as his main duty, then he does not know his job or is not equal to it, and he should be replaced by someone who is.

On the subject of competitiveness, it should be pointed out that the club president anxious to promote the welfare of the membership will devote much of his efforts toward minimizing the kind of competitive spirit that goes far to undermine the morale of camera-club members by distorting their objectives. For instead of working together, member is pitted against member and club against club in the scramble for ribbons, medals, and point scorings in general. Eagerness to win top place and to accumulate points leads to overemphasis on rewards, to the detriment of personal achievement and the weakening of personal integrity. To such an extent, in fact, that sometimes I find it hard to tell the difference between camera clubs and the commercial world. The coin of the club realm happens to be points instead of money; otherwise, the similarity is marked.

Particularly does the chairman need to make the most of a guest speaker who has something important to say. So-called "lectures," even at their best, can be greatly increased in value through audience participation, as in the case of the student–

teacher relationship (see Chapter 17, "New Patterns for Learning"). The story is told of one well-known speaker who started his "talk" with the question "Well, what do you want to know?" His audience, which had settled back to listen to a long monologue, was stunned for a few embarrassing moments. When they came to, they started firing questions as fast as the speaker could answer them. Of course, the talk was a huge success because everybody—speaker and audience—was in on it.

This formula will not always work. The nearest equivalent in a camera club is for the speaker to make a few introductory remarks to "set the stage," then invite questions. Whatever the method, whether this or the conventional one, where the speaker prefers to lecture first and answer questions afterward, the meeting chairman must be on his toes. He must make sure the lecture does not stay a lecture but is turned into a discussion from which, through the chairman's direction, the members get the maximum of help and inspiration.

CHAPTER TWENTY-ONE

The Babel of Labels

Some words fool you.

PHOTOGRAPHERS SURE MAKE a lot of trouble for themselves.
The matter appears simple enough. You make the kind of pictures you like to make in the way you like to make them. And
you don't care what anybody wants to call them—"pictorial"
or "documentary" or "modern" or what's-yours?

In fact, haven't you noticed that when you try to work in
one or another of these "styles," you almost invariably find
yourself working to a formula? But when you try to do nothing more than to make pictures, simply make pictures to please
yourself, then nomenclature vanishes and the resulting print
is uniquely your own expression—call it by any name you will.

Labels are a pitfall every photographer must guard against,
or become so lost in controversy that he loses sight of his main
objective—to nurture his capacity to understand and to develop
a personalized way of communicating his insight through photographs.

We have symposiums, discussions, debates—on "pictorialism" versus "the documentary," on the "modern approach,"
on "Is photography an art?" and endless variations on similar

242

themes. Confusion is added to confusion with such terms as "pictorial documentary" and "salon pictorialism." Even the term "reportage" is misinterpreted, with the sad result that nobody understands anybody else and one man's "art" becomes another man's "salon pictorialism."

If we must have a term, then perhaps "reportage" comes the nearest of all to describing a photographer's function, because at least the word implies communication of some kind: presenting in a photograph the interpretive report of a subject, the intelligent and thoughtful delineation of an idea, the reproduction of a mood observed, felt, and understood by the photographer.

Interpretation Counts Most

It is not the words we use but how we interpret them, each photographer for himself. Is pictorial photography, in its original sense of creative endeavor, so radically different from documentary photography that we can truly say the one is dead and only the other is alive? Actually, the two do not exclude each other to the extent so widely advertised and practiced. On the one hand—salon clichés, on the other—documentary preoccupations with social problems effectively close the minds of each side to the realities of living as an experience of the whole.

Both sides have been guilty of a misunderstanding and a misuse of the photographic medium as an instrument with limitless potentialities for saying things. Pictorialism, originally an outlet for original, that is, individual thought and feeling, has become "salon pictorialism," a shallow, pretentious, and surface substitute for real expression, its true possibilities overlooked, its opportunities hardly touched. The documentarian, with all life from which to choose material, too frequently selects only very narrow segments of it.

Both pictorialist and documentarian, therefore, appear to be in the wrong, but the latter would seem to be more right than the former, for at least he looks about him. He observes, tries to understand, does a little thinking and evaluating, makes real attempts to set down in pictures some kind of statement of what it all means to him. He may imitate, as most salon photographers do, but what he apes is another man's thinking. The salon worker is not even that lucky, for when he imitates, his models are only the static images of today's pictorialists.

Roy E. Stryker's explanation of the term "documentary" is gradually becoming generally accepted and appears to strike a balance between both camps. "It seems to be an erroneous idea that documentary pictures must be of the 'ash-can' school," he says, "that they must portray squalor or misery. To me, documentary is not synonymous with the tragic or the sordid, although such subject matter has its proportionate place, to the extent to which it occurs in life. Certainly the scenes at the country fair, the pictures that show town meetings in New England, even pictures of landscapes and industrial scenes should be part of the documentary entries."

Adams's Classification

Ansel Adams, the famous West Coast photographer, author, and lecturer, addressing a "documentary" group, once made a notable effort to resolve the whole matter of nomenclature as it relates to types of photographic activity. To clarify the issue of "pictorialism" versus "the documentary," both of which terms he held were meaningless except for their popular association with salons, on the one hand, and with a restricted point of view, on the other, Mr. Adams proposed the following classifications:

1. The simple record—microfile, passport pictures, and similar utilitarian photography.

2. Reportage, as represented in the work of newspaper and magazine photographers.

3. Illustration, such as commercial photography, standard portrait making, and other fields in which pictures are made to fit someone else's ideas and preferences.

4. Expressive photography.

The last group, according to Mr. Adams, would include all photography in which the worker attempts to express himself and range all the way from the mere snapshot made with a box camera by the immature photographer to the highest type of creative and interpretive photography. The difference lies only, he said, in the degree of intensity of thought, feeling, and imagination.

The fireworks started when W. Eugene Smith and Philippe Halsman, both famous for their work in photographic reportage, disagreed volubly with Adams's classification of reportage as a medium that is devoid of expressiveness. Adams had said that reportage is selective and objective only, that it does not interpret the subject matter photographed. Yes it does, said Smith and Halsman. It all depends on the photographer.

They felt that a photographer worth his salt uses every technical means at his command under a given set of circumstances to tell the story in the most effective way he knows. He expresses himself through selection and emphasis of one or another aspect of the material. He interprets the material by a choice of subject, viewpoint, lighting, arrangement, and the split-second recognition of the moment of greatest signifi-cance and revelation. The greater the photographer's under-standing, sensitivity, and technical facility to record his impres-sion, the more intelligent and revealing will be the message he presents.

The merely objective photographer, with only technical facility and no thought other than to cover the essential jour-nalistic features of the assignment, admittedly does not inter-pret, they submitted. But this does not prove that reportage is incapable of interpretation, of deep personal expression through a camera.

In defense of his views, Adams said he saw expressiveness at its highest in Alfred Stieglitz's "Equivalents" (a series of cloudscapes), Paul Strand's blades of grass, and Edward Wes-ton's rocks and sand. However, the opinion of the audience was that, excellent as these examples are in the creative sense, in essence they are no different in basic intent from the highest type of reportage. The sincerity of the honest photographer guides both. The only difference is in the choice of material and technical treatment. It was pointed out that the magazine photographer's message, because he uses familiar and human materials, will be more readily understandable and useful than the abstract expressions contained in pictures of grass, rock, and sand.

Adams used the occasion to make critical comments about both the documentarian and the pictorialist.

"The documentary is too closely identified with some political expedient, so that it has restricted itself to a certain aspect of society," he said. "It has not been very constructive. It is only two-dimensional, describing certain social conditions and presenting them without real evaluation of many of the most intrenched and evil aspects. Very seldom do we see the alternative in these pictures—the photographer's answer to the problem presented. Such photographs would have greater value if made more by implication of the conditions photographed than by bare fact."

He was even more critical of the pictorialists, who, he said, "have done everything they could to break down the creative potential of photography." He cited his experiences with salons in various cities throughout the country, in which he found a dead level of aimlessness and futility. In one city rich in photographic possibilities, the crop of pictures hung in the local salon gave so little inkling of the pictorially promising environment in which the photographers lived that the "pictures might have been made in a Pullman car."

Calling attention to the fact that there have never been so many people with the power to say something, Adams suggested that "ways and means be found to make more people express themselves through the camera in real, intense expressions." Though pictorialists as a group resisted his efforts to enlarge and intensify their photographic work, Adams said that he saw the nucleus of understanding in every group. Whenever he approached certain photographers individually, he was able to convince them, by showing them such pictures as those of Weston, Stieglitz, and Strand, that photography's ideals went far beyond the standards of the salon exhibition walls.

His mention of standards led to a number of efforts on the part of his audience to define the elements that make a picture universally acceptable. This is a matter of appreciation, it was held, and comes as a result of the level of general standards. As photographers improve their work, standards will gradually be

bettered, and poor pictures will be recognized for their inept-
ness and will be ignored.

"Modern Approach"

The confusion about terms led one camera club to assign
for its monthly competition the subject "pictures with a modern approach," without taking the trouble to explain what
the phrase meant. There was a reason: nobody in the club
really knew. As a result, only a small percentage of the entries
made any attempt to fulfill the assignment, the majority being
in the usual pictorial style. That more prints with "modern"—
loosely interpreted to mean documentary—qualities were not
submitted was attributed by club members to the fact that
they did not understand what was required.

It was apparent, as print after print was placed on the
easel for judging, that lack of a definition had thrown contributing members back to the salon type of work. With very
few prints of the "modern" type available, the judge was
obliged to consider the entries according to two standards—one,
"modern"; the other, "salon." In the first case, selection was
on the basis of originality and freshness of treatment; in the second, on print quality alone. The few who had made a sincere
effort to reflect their interest in contemporary life did succeed
in turning out pictures exhibiting a fair degree of aliveness.

The incident should have taught the club that you cannot
tell photographers how and what kind of pictures they should
make, that this is a personal matter with the photographer. But
it didn't. Nor did it occur to them that they were not thinking
of an "approach" but of subject matter only. As if the two were
separable.

Grierson's Interpretation

Modern photography was frankly described as "documentary" in a later talk to the same club by Samuel Grierson, veteran pictorialist and salon exhibitor. The term referred, he said, to "a good photograph of an interesting subject of the times in which the photographer lives." Also, he added, the print should be technically well done, but in straightforward manner, without other than routine darkroom manipulations.

His attempt to clarify his meaning of modernity in picture making was stated in terms of pictorialism. Although he represents a sort of middle ground between the documentarians and the salon pictorialists, his philosophy of photography is nearer that of the first than of the second. Followed through intelligently, it could well prove the starting point for a reform in pictorialism which would raise salon work to a higher level, perhaps one that might attract the efforts of the better photographers.

Photography is the most modern of all the arts in point of time, Grierson elaborated, and it should, therefore, be kept in its time. This does not mean that documentaries of old, broken-down buildings are the only pictures that may be termed "modern." Modernity does not imply the narrow point of view in which only the disagreeable aspects of life must be shown. A modern picture can also depict life in a first-class neighborhood, which can be documented just as well as the slums.

There is a document in every aspect and on every level of life and circumstances, he said. To go modern, one does not need to restrict oneself to one level and to one condition of existence in the life of the community. Nor do pictures have to be "socially significant" or expose poor conditions. This is only one phase of the world we live in. There are many others. To the seeing, understanding photographer, all levels offer interesting and valuable camera material.

Grierson's analysis actually side-stepped the whole issue of terminology and developed into an appeal for honesty and personal conviction in picture making.

He denounced such phony salon favorites as costume portraits in which the subject is dressed in the clothes of a past era, representing someone no longer alive. He advised photographers to take subjects as they found them, in authentic dress, manners, and environment, not as actors portraying a role unsuited to their characters. If you find a subject in a saloon, don't order him into the parlor and dress him up to look like something out of the history books, he said. The picture will be unconvincing, arty, and pointless. Rely on portraying the character of the individual, not on tricks and masquerades.

Only Good and Bad Pictures

Talks of this kind help to clarify the issue of nomenclature, help to explain the differences between "styles" of photography, try to show that in the last analysis there really are no differences. Only good pictures and bad pictures. Only pictures that mean something and pictures that don't mean anything. Only pictures that are real expressions and pictures that are empty.

Labels may hamper a photographer's free expression. For example, take a recent show of the New York Press Photographers Association, where a "pictorial" class was listed along with classes for spot news, sports, speedlight, features, portraits, and personalities.

It is significant that in the few examples where press photographers effectively adopted the pictorial approach, their success was due largely to their ability to see subject matter with the directness that characterized their news pictures. Where, however, the photographers became consciously pictorial, their pictures were dull, vague, and less sincere. The salon pictorialist depends more on technique than on subject matter, whereas the press photographer's opportunities lie in the exploitation of his natural inclination to portray the essence of contemporary life.

Photography is a way of thinking, an expression of environment, tempo, conviction, and purpose. The newsman does not think in pictorial terms, and when he tries to do so, he gives himself a handicap he cannot always overcome. He is at his best when working under the pressure of things happening. The salon pictorialist's attitude is neither familiar nor suitable for the news cameraman, whether he is photographing spot-news material or trying his hand at pictorial subjects.

The fact that news pictures in any category possess an aliveness that salon prints frequently lack made the exhibition a valuable object lesson for amateur photographers who wanted to get freshness into their work. Particularly useful was a study of the prize-winning pictorials, all of which said something, specifically and dramatically. Although they maintained the quiet atmosphere of the pictorial approach, the news photographers gave their pictures interest by introducing in the straightforward style of the news shot such qualities as incident, excitement, and the atmosphere of a living experience.

CHAPTER TWENTY-TWO

Photography as Art

*All I have learned about photography, I have
learned through painting.*

HENRI CARTIER-BRESSON

As THE PROS AND CONS whether photography may be truly
called an art dart back and forth across the decades since
Daguerre, the conviction is steadily growing, though with
exceeding slowness in some quarters, that photography is undoubtedly an art, but only when the photographer is an artist.
And is not this true of any of the media conventionally accepted
as art?

In the same sense that we call a man an artist (as distinguished, of course, from the routine use of the term to
designate anyone who uses pen, pencil, brush, or other tool, to
delineate or amend an image of any sort) who is sufficiently
endowed with imaginative and creative gifts to produce what
is generally agreed to be a work of art, so too in the case of
the artist–photographer.

What is an artist? An individual of uncommon sensi-
bility, who is responsive to the nuances of mood, substance, and
situation he encounters in the world around him; who pene-

trates surface appearances and values to the meanings that lie below and even beyond the subject itself. Because he has a developed sense of awareness, things are not merely things, but become the revelations of experience thought, felt, and observed and finally communicated as a personal discovery to anyone who takes the time to look appreciatively at the resulting photograph.

I submit that a photographer endowed with similar artistic instinct and ability can produce photographs on the same level. Incidentally, I insist, despite prevailing opinions to the contrary, that such qualities can be developed (to a degree) given the congenial atmosphere of a teacher–student relationship in which both share cooperatively in the growing process (see Chapter 17, "New Patterns for Learning"), the teacher in a sympathetic attempt to call forth whatever latent talent he may perceive in the student, the latter in trying to keep his mind open to the new world being opened up to him.

In the numerous, usually dead-end, panel discussions on the status of photography as an art, the familiar distinction is made that photography is mechanical because a mechanical instrument is the medium involved. This attitude ignores entirely the fact that back of the instrument, the camera, is a human intelligence, reacting, like the artist's, to the subject material at hand.

The physical result is different, of course, but the depth of perceptivity need not be. Painter and photographer may actually say the same thing, each in a way conditioned by the medium in which he works. Or they may say different things, one as profound as the other. Because of the characteristics of the medium involved, one may even make a statement not possible to the other.

Selection

By the strictures of the idiom in which he works, the photographer must exercise the element of selection far more specifically than the painter. He cannot recall from memory, as the painter can, a particular lighting, subject angle, a gesture, movement, expression, a desirable disposition of subject elements. They must be present in front of his camera. Thus, if the lighting is not right, he comes back when it is; if the mood is not appropriate, he waits for a change; if the situation lacks significance, he waits until something happens to give it depth and meaning. Like the painter, he selects, and the result is judged, by himself as well as by others, by the quality of thought and feeling revealed in that selection.

Photography is unique as an art medium. It is neither comparable to nor competitive with painting, drawing, or any other image-making technique. An optical-chemical method of producing pictures by the agency of light impinging on a silver emulsion, the photograph is a product of subject choice (representing the artist's visual experience), exposure of film to light by mechanically controlled devices, and the optical-chemical processing of the result into the final picture.

One of the strongest proofs, if proof be needed, that photography can inspire, and implement, artistic impulses, where such are present, is that in countless instances persons engaged in the arts of painting, drawing, etc. have turned to photography as a second, if not a substitute, medium of expression. In most cases the convert has found in the new medium a completely fresh approach to communicating his visual experience, not necessarily "better" than he could, say as a painter, but in a way perhaps more appropriate to the material in question.

The Approaches Differ

Whether they abandon painting in favor of the camera or continue working in both fields, painter–photographers generally agree that each is an art in its own right, with a uniquely characteristic manner of self-expression.

Charles Sheeler, who has achieved eminence in both arts, stated the matter cogently to his biographer, Constance Rourke:

"I have come to value photography more and more for those things which it alone can accomplish rather than to discredit it for the things which can only be achieved through another medium. In painting I have had a continued interest in natural forms and have sought the best use of them for the enhancement of design. In photography I have strived to enhance my technical equipment for the best statement of the immediate facts."

As the youngest of the arts, photography still is trying, after six-score years since its invention, to get a secure foothold on the level of recognition accorded the older forms of creative work. Although photography as an art continues to be a relatively strange language beyond the circle of its devotees, there are signs of a growing general appreciation.

One of the the most encouraging developments in this direction is the changing attitude of art museums toward photographic exhibitions. Not only is there a steadily increasing number of such shows in museums which never had them before, but curators have become more discriminating. Those who used to hang the pseudo-artistic efforts of the camera club "salonists" are learning to appreciate the difference between the pretense, the half-baked emotion, and the honest artistic achievement.

CHAPTER TWENTY-THREE

Where to, Photographer?

A sustained interest, a sense of continuity, is essential to get the most out of picture making. Photography becomes part of the process of growing. You reach out for more as you understand more. More things assume importance. As a result your pictures become better because of this inner growth.

EDWARD STEICHEN

YOU TAKE IT FROM HERE.

It's high time to make pictures instead of talking about them. But before you pick up your camera, better chart your course. Where are you headed, photographer?

I hope the talk back there in the book will help you decide.

First, you establish a viewpoint, try to formulate a valid reason for taking pictures. It has to be a personal reason, one based on the things you are—*your* background, *your* likes and dislikes, *your* way of seeing, understanding, appreciating, evaluating. In short, your pictures must reflect *your* personality, not another's.

Only thus will your pictures be uniquely your own—

"unique" because you see them in a special way, though not necessarily "original" in the narrow sense of the term.

When you know what you want to do in photography—to describe people and their ways, to show the meanings hidden in ordinary objects, to reveal an appreciation of the many facets that make up your world—the rest is a matter of circumstance and know-how. You photograph what you see in the best way you can and acquire new techniques as you need them to express yourself in pictures.

You must have something to say, then say what you mean with the words of photography, the techniques. A photograph without purpose—one based, for example, on a pictorial cliché—will carry little personal meaning. It will be a mechanical copy; that is, not your own statement but somebody else's. You won't be happy with it.

If techniques are words, then you can use them to say anything you want in photography and use the same techniques-words to say different things. These "words" of photography are part of a lexicon from which you select the combinations of phrases you need to say specific things with a camera.

Much of the confusion among amateur photographers concerning the use of basic techniques is due to the fact that writers and teachers go over the fundamentals every time a new application is described; whereas, in fact, if techniques are learned like words in a dictionary, on the basis of what each technique is intended to accomplish (how to light a subject to show texture, for example), the photographer will be more likely to think of subject matter creatively. He will place the emphasis where it belongs—on the thinking and feeling behind the picture, on the picture idea itself.

A given technique will do a certain job, and it will do that job the same way every time. The difference between applications of the technique will be in the meaning conveyed, not in the technical results.

Photographs are made of light, mood, texture, form, and line, as I have tried to point out in Part 2 of this book. These elements are used to make pictures of children, landscapes, portraits, still lifes, sports, or anything else. Within each element lies a body of specific techniques. Where and how you use them is your personal affair and nobody else's.

The same techniques in the hands of two different photographers may result in a static image by the one and a significant image by the other. The value of techniques lies in how they are used. Techniques by themselves are barren. To come alive with meaning, they must be employed interpretively. That's where you come in.

Photography has limitless potentialities for every user of the camera. Only rarely, however, are these potentialities realized among contemporary amateurs. The fault lies with the stress on techniques in schools, in exhibitions, in the camera clubs, in photographic literature, and with the deplorable lack of imaginative leadership. Here and there, however, are hopeful signs, some of which are indicated in the third part of this book.

Every photographer can help to make these signs into actualities. How about it, reader? Will you lend a hand?